MW00462495

IMAGES
of America

BREAKHEART
RESERVATION

This c. 1900 image shows Howlett's Mill on the Saugus River, adjacent to present-day Breakheart Reservation. The mill was named after John Howlett, who operated it as a snuff mill from 1837 to 1871. It was then used as a sawmill until 1902. Use of this site dates back to 1662, when John Gifford established an ironworks here after leaving his position as second agent for the nearby Saugus Iron Works at Hammersmith. (Courtesy of Judith Loubris McCarthy.)

ON THE COVER: Members of the Lynn Historical Society gather at Breakheart Hill Camp in October 1898. From left to right are (first row) Nathan M. Hawkes, Charles J.H. Woodberry, William S. Burrill, and Howard M. Newhall; (second row) Charles H. Newhall (holding hat), Luther S. Johnson, Henry F. Tapley (hand across chest), Benjamin F. Spinney, John L. Parker (wearing black bowler hat), and Wilbur F. Newhall (seated below Parker); (third row) Benjamin N. Johnson (co-owner of the Breakheart Hill Forest), James S. Newhall (hatless with white beard), and John S. Bartlett (holding post, co-owner of Breakheart Hill Forest). Later that day, the party rode through Lynn Woods in a tallyho coach. (Photograph by George S. Bliss; courtesy of Edward W. Patterson Jr.)

IMAGES
of America

BREAKHEART
RESERVATION

Alison C. Simcox and Douglas L. Heath

ARCADIA
PUBLISHING

Copyright © 2013 by Alison C. Simcox and Douglas L. Heath
ISBN 978-0-7385-9779-9

Published by Arcadia Publishing
Charleston, South Carolina

Printed in the United States of America

Library of Congress Control Number: 2012941483

For all general information, please contact Arcadia Publishing:
Telephone 843-853-2070
Fax 843-853-0044
E-mail sales@arcadiapublishing.com
For customer service and orders:
Toll-Free 1-888-313-2665

Visit us on the Internet at www.arcadiapublishing.com

Benjamin Newhall Johnson pauses while riding his horse, Duke, along the shore of Upper Pond (now Silver Lake) in December 1931. This was one of Johnson's last rides in his beloved forest, as he died only two months later on February 19, 1932. More than any other person, Johnson is credited with creating Breakheart Hill Forest and ensuring its preservation for future generations. (Photograph by Sanborn; courtesy of Lynn Museum and Historical Society.)

CONTENTS

ACKNOWLEDGMENTS

Many people helped make this book possible. First, we thank Judith Loubris McCarthy for providing many photographs of her family, the Parkers, who lived at Breakheart Hill Farm at the park's entrance. Judith's great-great-grandfather was caretaker for the farm and gatekeeper to Breakheart Hill Forest when it was the private retreat of wealthy Lynn businessmen. Sean Fisher, archivist at the Massachusetts Department of Conservation and Recreation (DCR), offered his time and expertise and identified people in photographs who otherwise would have remained nameless. Edward Patterson Jr., former park ranger at Camp Nihan and president of the Saugus Historical Society, shared his collection of photographs in his home in Ossipee, New Hampshire. James Nihan kindly allowed us to use a photograph of his grandparents, George and Annie Nihan, and Malcolm Patterson Jr., dean at Endicott College, allowed us to scan his remarkable album of photographs taken by his father, a "CCC boy" at Breakheart in the 1930s. Don Young, longtime freelance photographer for the *Wakefield Daily Item*, contributed photographs of camping trips in Breakheart and of the lunar eclipse 1963 as seen from Castle Hill. Maria Caniglia, Bill Dalton, and Tony Gutro of the DCR always welcomed us at the Breakheart Visitor Center and gave us access to the center's collection of Native American artifacts, photographs, and Civilian Conservation Corps memorabilia.

Wakefield's Beebe Memorial Library, Lynn and Saugus Public Libraries, Wakefield Department of Public Works (DPW), Robert S. Peabody Museum of Archaeology, Frances Loeb Library of Harvard University's Graduate School of Design, Lynn Museum and Historical Society (LHS), New England Orienteering Club, and Saugus Historical Society also generously lent us materials from their collections. Special thanks go to Steven Babbitt (LHS); Todd Baldwin (Wakefield DPW); Sally Rege Carroll; Rick Dawe of the Lynn Water and Sewer Commission; Joe Gentleman (Southern Essex Registry of Deeds); Jim Comeau, Alexander Gillman, Tony Hart, Mike Nelson, and Charlie Petrucci (DCR); Joseph P. Kopera (Massachusetts Geological Survey); Dan Burgess and Joan LeBlanc (Saugus River Watershed Council); and Annette Murray (Friends of Breakheart Reservation). Finally, we thank Katie McAlpin and Ryan Easterling, our editors at Arcadia Publishing, and, as always, our sons Ian and Alec.

INTRODUCTION

Breakheart Reservation is a 640-acre scenic area of woodlands and hilly terrain containing two lakes and a section of the Saugus River. There are seven hills with views that, on a clear day, stretch south to the Blue Hills, west to Mount Wachusett, north to New Hampshire, and east to the Atlantic Ocean.

Geologically, Breakheart is on the northern edge of the Boston Basin, which is a low area of slates and mudstones. The uplands north of the Boston Basin are composed of metamorphic and igneous rocks. In Breakheart, these rocks are mainly quartzites (metamorphosed beach sands) that formed from 912 to 606 million years ago (late Precambrian) and volcanic rocks that formed from eruptions almost 600 million years ago (also late Precambrian). However, the geological features most evident at Breakheart are from a much more recent time, the last glacial period called the Wisconsin, which extended from about 110,000 to 10,000 years ago. Like all areas of New England, bedrock at Breakheart was glacially sculpted, with striations on rocks that show ice flow direction. Where bedrock is not at the surface, it is covered by glacial till, a mixture of rock material ranging from clay to boulders, and outwash sediments. Breakheart also has a striking number of glacier-transported erratic boulders, some nearly as large as houses, and cliffs formed by glacial plucking, which occurs when ice moves over a bedrock outcrop and plucks rock off the back wall.

Archaeological evidence shows that the first people, called Paleo-Indians, moved into New England about 11,000 years ago. They hunted mastodon, caribou, and other tundra animals using spears with fluted points, which have been found on hilltops, the sides of valleys, and the shores of glacial lakes throughout the Northeast. By 9,000 years ago, hardwood trees, such as beech, oak, and maple, began to appear, and wetlands provided rich habitat for plants, birds, deer, and other animals. This period of plentiful food resources and increasing human population is called the Early Archaic.

Fluted and projectile points and other artifacts from the Archaic Period (10,000 to 3,000 years ago) have been found at sites in Wakefield and Saugus, including the Mill River, a tributary of the Saugus River less than a mile from Breakheart. Evidence suggests that early people spent summers near the coast and traveled inland up the Saugus River to camp during the winter. By the Late Archaic, Native Americans had developed additional tools for hunting, including fish weirs, and began making pottery and growing squash and gourds. They also began settling in campsites, and trading became more important. In the Woodland period that followed (about 1,000 BC to the arrival of Europeans in the early 17th century), villages grew in size and number and, by the Late Woodland period, people were growing maize and beans.

According to the National Park Service, when European settlement began in the 1600s, Native Americans in the Saugus area were part of a loose confederation called the Pawtucket or Penacook Indians, with a population of about 20,000. In a 1918 lecture to the Lynn Historical Society, Fred Terrell, an amateur archaeologist, spoke about a "pestilence among the Indians" in 1616, 1617, and 1619 that killed about nine-tenths of the native population. Historians now believe this pestilence may have been the bubonic plague, which was introduced by European fishermen along the Maine coast and spread to Rhode Island. So when Puritans arrived north of Boston in the 1620s, most Native Americans were already gone. King Philip's War in 1675 and 1676 resulted in the conquest or enslavement of the remaining population.

In 1630, the Saugus territory included present-day towns of Swampscott, Nahant, Lynn, Saugus, Lynnfield, Wakefield, and Reading. In 1637, the legislature renamed the territory Lin or Lynn. Soon after, colonists began to settle along the Saugus River, which had been called "Abousett" by Native Americans. In 1901, Nathan Mortimer Hawkes, author of local history books, imagined the scene when colonists arrived: "When the first settlers discovered this strath, encircled by rocky hills, a dense forest of pine covered its surface. The brook meandered through meadows carpeted with the uncounted pine needles, over which the simple red man noiselessly glided in pursuit of game. His wigwam was ever near a running stream not always a water-way that would float his birch bark canoe, but such a stream as fish could swim in, that he could lose his foot-prints in, if haply hostile intruders threatened."

The settlers harvested fish, including alewives, bass, and silver eels, and built gristmills and sawmills. For iron tools and utensils, they relied on shipments from England. However, when the Great Migration from England to the American colonies ended about 1640, fewer ships came to New England and iron products became scarce. To address this shortage, the General Court of the Massachusetts Bay Colony enacted an ordinance in 1641 for "encouragement to discovery of mines." John Winthrop Jr., son of the colony's governor, sailed to England and found about two dozen men willing to invest in a "Company of Undertakers of the Iron Works in New England." He returned in 1643 with skilled workmen and established an ironworks on the Saugus River to process bog iron, which operated from 1646 to 1670 (now the Saugus Iron Works National Historic Site). The ironworks' first general agent was Richard Leader, followed in 1651 by John Gifford. But Gifford became embroiled in controversy and lawsuits and left in 1662 to found his own ironworks.

Gifford chose a site about two miles up the Saugus River. At this time, both ironworks sites were part of the West Parish of Lynn. It was not until 1815 that this parish became "Saugus," the original Native American name for the land now comprising Lynn and Saugus. Gifford's ironworks was adjacent to land that, in the next century, became known as the Six Hundred Acres and later Breakheart Hill Forest. The ironworks operated until about 1675. Subsequently, a sawmill was built on or near the site (1703–1740), which was converted into a wire-manufacturing operation (1814–1828) and snuff-grinding mill (1837–1871), before being used again as a sawmill (1871–1902). From 1837 until it collapsed during a 1907 storm, the mill was known as Howlett's Mill.

The story of the Six Hundred Acres began on April 15, 1706, when a Lynn town meeting established a committee "to Divide all the Undivided Common Lands within the Towne of Lynn." These lands included Nahant and "the great range of woodland in the north of the town." The committee obtained a list of people living in these areas in 1705 and devised rules for dividing the land "according to what each proprietor and Inhabitant have of Lands upon said List." The common lands were laid out in seven divisions; the First Division to the west of Saugus River became known as the Six Hundred Acres.

According to Alonzo Lewis in *The History of Lynn including Nahant*, "The woodlands were laid out in Ranges, forty rods [660 feet] in width, and these were divided into lots containing from about one eighth of an acre to eight acres." In September 1706, the town considered "the great difficulty of laying out highways on the common lands, by reason of the swamps, hills, and rockenes of the land, theirfore voated, that . . . every person interested therein, shall have free liberty at all times, to pass and repass over each others' lotts of lands, to fetch their wood and such other things as shall be upon their lands. . . provided they do not cut downe any sort of tree or trees in their so passing over."

Among the notable families that owned land in the Six Hundred Acres were Hones, Hawkes, Hitchings, Edmands, Alley, Cheever, Wiley, Floyd, Pratt, White, and Newhall. During the 18th and early 19th centuries, most of the land was used for wood supplies, although it included tillable land in the east and south that became farms. At that time, most things needed for daily life were produced at home or could be obtained from (or sold to) local mills, and traveling any distance meant an arduous journey.

Many early roads were old Indian trails passable by foot or, if improved, by horseback or two-wheeled carts pulled by oxen. Until 1763, when Forest Street was laid out, there were no cart roads at all through the Six Hundred Acres. Forty years later, however, a road was built along the eastern boundary of the Six Hundred Acres that hinted at a future beyond the dreams of the colonists. This was the straight Newburyport Turnpike (now US Route 1), which was built to connect markets in Boston to Newburyport. But building this road was far from simple. According to a 2007 article in *Wicked Local Saugus*, "The topography of the new road was very challenging with intervening hills, valleys, bogs, woodlands, marshes, steep rocks, and waterways. Swamps were filled, ledges were blasted, bridges were built out of stone and nine hills had to be removed in order to complete the job." In the early days, the road was considered a failure and financial burden and, for a century, was too rough for all but the hardiest of travelers.

While areas outside cities were still mainly farming communities, by the mid-19th century, cities had become crowded and polluted. From about 1870 to 1930, it was popular for wealthy people to build rustic-style retreats along lakes and rivers in wooded areas. Instead of traveling to New Hampshire or Maine, three prominent men from Lynn, attorney Benjamin Johnson, banker Micajah Clough, and shoe manufacturer John Bartlett, decided to develop a retreat in the nearby Six Hundred Acres. They established the Breakheart Hill Forestry Company as a vehicle for purchasing land. The name "Breakheart" was adopted from the name of a hill in the Six Hundred Acres, which was mentioned in Daniel Hitching's will of 1781. Starting with 14 acres in 1891, Johnson and his partners eventually enlarged their holdings to 644 acres. They called their retreat Breakheart Hill Forest, built a hunting lodge called Breakheart Hill Camp, developed bridal paths, and dammed swamps to create two lakes. For many years, the three families shared the forest, and prominent men from Lynn visited for outings.

In 1900, an event occurred that suddenly put Breakheart in the headlines. On October 8, 1900, the hired caretaker of Breakheart, George E. Bailey, was brutally murdered by John C. Best, a farmhand from New Brunswick. Reporters and others flocked to Breakheart Hill Farm, the scene of the crime. Two years later, Best was electrocuted at Charlestown State Prison.

Between 1891 and 1933, Johnson and his partners bought 55 parcels through the Breakheart Hill Forestry. In 1934, as they had wished, their executors sold the property to the Metropolitan District Commission (MDC) to be preserved for future generations. The timing coincided with Franklin Roosevelt's Civilian Conservation Corps (CCC) program for employing young men, so the MDC turned Breakheart over to the federal government to set up a CCC camp. Over a six-year period, CCC boys built roads, developed trails and picnic areas, planted trees, and restored the dams for the Upper and Lower Ponds, resulting in the reservation much as we know it today. Their forest restoration efforts also resulted in an increase in wildlife, including beaver, fishers, coyote, blue heron, and owls. In 1961, after being closed to the public for over 60 years, Breakheart Reservation was finally opened to the public.

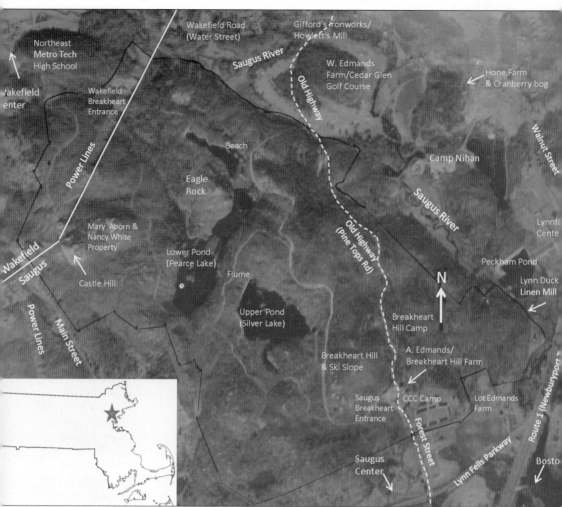

Northeast
Metro Tech
High School

Wakefield
enter

Wakefield
Breakheart
Entrance

Power Lines

Wakefield

Saugus

Castle Hill

Mary Aborn &
Nancy White
Property

Power Lines

Main Street

Wakefield Road
(Water Street)

Saugus River

Beach

Eagle
Rock

Lower Pond
(Pearce Lake)

Flume

Upper Pond
(Silver Lake)

Gifford's Ironworks/
Howlett's Mill

Old Highway

W. Edmands
Farm/Cedar Glen
Golf Course

Camp Nihan

Saugus River

Old Highway
(Pine Tops Rd)

N

Breakheart
Hill Camp

Breakheart Hill
& Ski Slope

A. Edmands/
Breakheart Hill Farm

Saugus
Breakheart
Entrance

CCC Camp

Forest Street

Saugus
Center

Hone Farm
& Cranberry bog

Walnut Street

Lynnfi
Cente

Peckham Pond

Lynn Duck
Linen Mill

Lot Edmands
Farm

Route 1 (Newburyport)

Lynn Fells Parkway

Bosto

This reference map shows the location of many features discussed in this book. The base map is from an aerial photograph taken in December 1938. This may be the oldest aerial image of Breakheart Reservation, and it is probably part of a series made to survey damage from the hurricane of September 21, 1938. (Courtesy of Wakefield Department of Public Works.)

One

Prehistory to Colonial Settlement

Breakheart Reservation lies in an area underlain by bedrock formed over millions of years. The rocks record a complex past, including uplift and folding associated with the creation of the Appalachian Mountains. The most recent major event to mark the landscape was the Wisconsin glaciation (extending from about 110,000 to 10,000 years ago) when thick ice covered most of Canada, the Midwest, and New England. By 14,000 years ago, the ice front had receded to a location near the present northern border of Massachusetts, leaving a landscape covered with glacial till, pocked by kettle ponds, and littered with boulders (called erratics). The land surface was also cut by meltwater streams, including the ancestral Saugus River, which today meanders through Wakefield, Lynnfield, and Saugus (including Breakheart) before emptying into the Atlantic Ocean at Lynn.

As outlined in the introduction, archaeologists have found evidence that people camped, hunted, and fished along the Saugus (or Abousett) River for thousands of years beginning with Paleo-Indians and continuing through the Archaic and Woodland periods. Native Americans in the Saugus area were part of a loose confederation called the Pawtucket or Penacook Indians. When the first Europeans made their way up the Saugus River in the early 1600s, they found a forested landscape with areas already cleared and cultivated by these native people. The settlers harvested fish, including alewives and eels, built gristmills and sawmills, and, in 1646, established the nation's first integrated ironworks, which included a blast furnace, forge, and rolling mill, on the Saugus River at the head of the tidewater. The ironworks' second general agent, John Gifford, left amidst disputes with the company's creditors and managers and founded an ironworks two miles upstream beside a tract of common land in what was then the West Parish of Lynn. In 1706, this rugged and rocky land was divided among male settlers and became known as the Six Hundred Acres. Throughout the 18th and 19th centuries, as land around it was developed and adapted to various uses, the Six Hundred Acres (now Breakheart Reservation) remained virtually unchanged, save for harvesting of its wood.

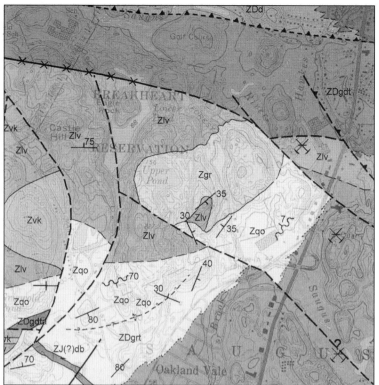

Joseph P. Kopera of the Massachusetts Geologic Survey produced this map of Breakheart Reservation and vicinity in 2011. Formed 912 to 606 million years ago, the Westboro Quartzite (Zqo) in the southern part of Breakheart is the oldest rock unit in the area. The Lynn Volcanics (Zlv, about 596 million years old) overlie the Westboro formation and the Dedham Granite (Zgr, about 630 million years old). (Courtesy of Joseph P. Kopera.)

The Westboro Quartzite originated as sand in a shallow sea over 600 million years ago. This outcrop of Westboro Quartzite, located near Breakheart's visitor center, was dubbed "the plowshare" by geologist Richard Hogan in 1935. Its impressive glacial striations were preserved because they were buried by glacial till until 1938, when the till was used to reconstruct the entrance to Breakheart. The striations are oriented from northwest to southeast, indicating ice flow direction. (Authors' collection.)

This large boulder, or erratic, is located beside Hemlock Road in Breakheart. It is one of many rocks carried by thick ice over the landscape. As the ice melted some 14,000 years ago, entrained or rafted boulders dropped onto the ground at various distances from their origin. (Authors' collection.)

This semi-legible signature, carved in 1900 on Castle Hill, may be the oldest inscription in the exposed rocks at Breakheart. Such carvings are rare in the park because the public had limited access before 1934, and the hard, granular bedrock throughout the park is difficult to carve. (Authors' collection.)

Five hundred years ago, the shores along the Saugus River may have contained one or more Native American settlements or winter camps similar to the one shown in this diorama of a Pawtucket village beside the Merrimack River. Daily life focused on activities such as planting (including corn and beans), hunting and fishing, preparing food, and making tools. (Courtesy of Robert S. Peabody Museum of Archaeology.)

Native Americans camped along the Saugus River, spending summers near the coast and moving inland during winter months. They built their shelters, or wigwams, with saplings arranged in a circle, bending them to form an arch at the top. The arch was then covered with mats of bullrush leaves. (Courtesy of DCR.)

This image features a prehistoric set of tools found in the Breakheart area. These were flaked into a rough core, or preform, and then shaped by grinding or abrading with other stones. The tip of a deer's antler, or tine, was used to break off flakes and chips from a larger stone, commonly jasper, in a process called pressure flaking. (Courtesy of DCR.)

These artifacts, which include spear tips and projectile points, have ages ranging over thousands of years (8,000 to 450 years). All were found within Breakheart Reservation or along the Saugus River or its tributary, the Mill River. Native Americans used jasper, a type of chert, from a local quarry for making tools because this rock easily chips into sharp edges. (Courtesy of DCR.)

These green heart trade beads are from the 1600s to early 1700s. Beads such as these were called wampum, a shortened form of the Massachusett or Narragansett word wampumpeag, meaning "white strings [of shell beads]." Native Americans collected oblong shells, which they polished and sawed into beads. While native people did not use wampum as money, colonists, lacking hard money, used it as a medium of exchange. (Courtesy of DCR.)

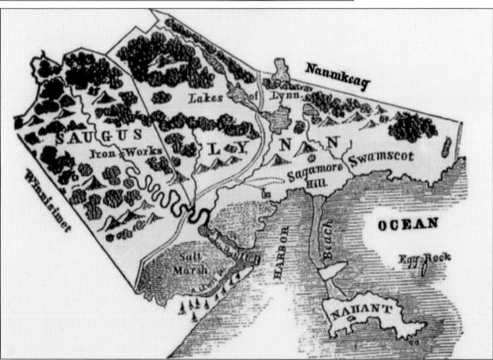

This map of Lynn and Surroundings by Clarence W. Hobbs (1886) shows the coastal setting and basic landscape features of the area. Note the easy access for Native Americans and colonial settlers from the coast to the Breakheart area, located along the Saugus River just upstream of the ironworks. Naumkeag is the Native American name for Salem, and Winnisimet is the former name of Chelsea. (Courtesy of Beebe Memorial Library.)

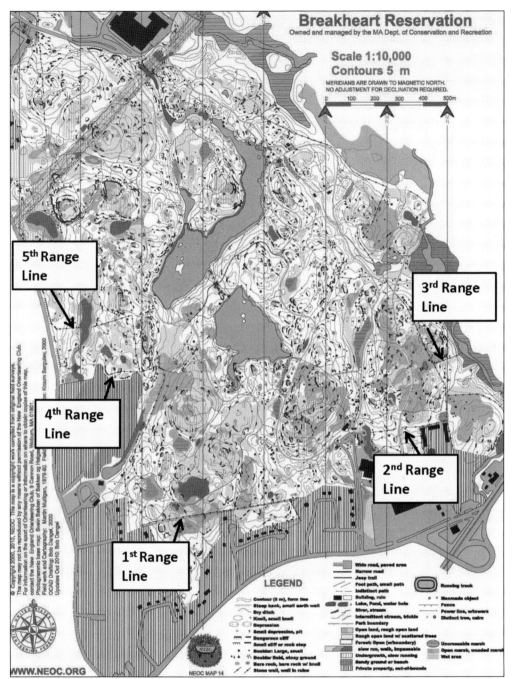

This detailed map of Breakheart Reservation shows trails, bedrock outcrops, and old stone walls, which were part of the eight range lines that defined the 1706 boundaries of the Six Hundred Acres. The range lines were 40 rods (660 feet) apart. (Breakheart Reservation map, copyright 2010, reproduced with permission of New England Orienteering Club.)

This stone wall is part of the second range line of the original Six Hundred Acres and marked the northern boundary of an 18-acre property that was owned by Daniel Hitchings in the 1700s. After many exchanges of ownership, this property became Breakheart Hill Farm in 1892. This wall lies just east of Breakheart's visitor center. (Authors' collection.)

Breakheart's agrarian past can be seen in the stone walls that crisscross the park, marking range lines, old property boundaries and pastures, climbing up and down hills, and even crossing land that is now submerged. Colonists called the stones that littered their land "fieldstones" or sometimes "hardheads" or "cobbles." In the 1700s and 1800s, much of Breakheart was deforested for firewood, and animals that depended on forest habitat became rare. (Authors' collection.)

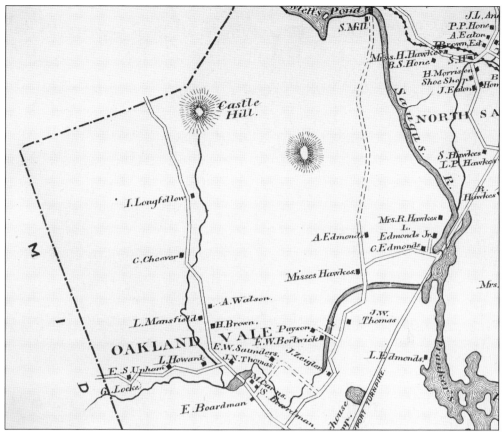

The 18th century "Old Highway," shown as a dashed line on an 1884 map, ran from Artemas Edmands's farm to Howlett's Pond. Part of the Old Highway still crosses Cedar Glen Golf Club (below). In 1907, Nathan Hawkes wrote, "There is an old road that leads out by Hewlett's mill, a mile beyond. It is a picturesque scene that meets the eye of the bold stroller who ventures up this region, which may be haunted by the shade of 'old Bill Edmands.' There are rocks and rills well worth seeing. There are abandoned apple orchards, vainly struggling with native trees for possession. Not a vestige of the buildings where the pugnacious Mr. Edmands lived can be seen. The cellar where he stored his potatoes and horsed his barrels of cider, the New England farmer's beverage, can scarcely be distinguished from a last year's woodchuck's hole." (Above, courtesy of Lynn Museum and Historical Society; below, authors' collection.)

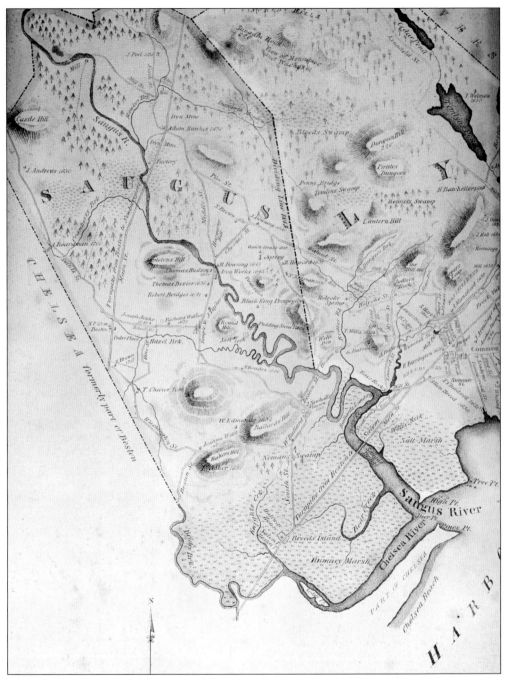

This 1829 map of Lynn and Saugus by Alonzo Lewis, published by Pendleton's Lithography of Boston, shows the Saugus River from Breakheart to the Atlantic Ocean. The map shows a forested landscape with extensive coastal marshes, inland swamps, and tributary streams and dotted with rounded hills. The map also shows houses of original settlers, mills, and roads, including the Newburyport and the Boston to Salem Turnpikes. (Courtesy of Lynn Museum and Historical Society.)

Two

MILLS ON THE SAUGUS RIVER

The Saugus River provided a route for Native Americans to travel inland in canoes to camp during the winter. When Puritan settlers moved inland from Lynn in the 1600s, they followed old Indian trails along the river. They would have met few Native Americans, however, because most had already died from disease introduced by European fishermen. After finding a place to settle, colonists began building houses and planting crops. Most farms were subsistence farms, producing a little extra to trade in nearby towns. Some settlers established mills, which exerted a strong influence on the well being of the surrounding area. The Saugus River had many saw, grist and corn mills that provided raw material for the settlers' food and shelter, but it also had mills that produced less essential products like cider, chocolate, coffee, and snuff. In fact, in the late 18th to mid-19th centuries, Saugus became renowned for its snuff industry.

Iron tools and utensils were also essential, but after the Great Migration of the 1630s, iron products were scarce. In response, John Winthrop Jr., son of the Massachusetts Bay Colony governor, established an ironworks on the Saugus River in 1646 to process bog iron (now the Saugus Iron Works National Historic Site). The ironwork's second general agent, John Gifford, became embroiled in arguments and lawsuits and even landed in jail for a few years. In 1662, Gifford paid 200 pounds sterling to Thomas Breedon of Boston for 260 acres along the Saugus River beside present-day Breakheart Reservation and established his own ironworks. He operated the ironworks until 1675 when the economic disruption caused by King Philip's War forced him to close. Over the years, Gifford's site became a sawmill (1703–1740), a wire-manufacturing operation (1814–1828), a snuff grinding mill (1837–1871), and, once again, a sawmill (1871–1902).

In 1814, just downstream from Gifford's site, another historic milldam was established. This fieldstone dam, which still exists in Breakheart, provided power for the Linen and Duck Manufactory Company of Boston. This mill stopped operating after the War of 1812, when the cost and demand for sailcloth declined.

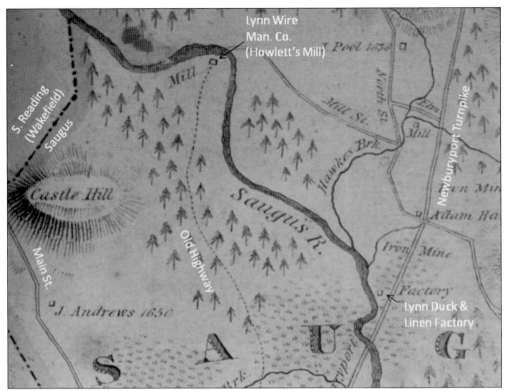

This 1829 map of Lynn and Saugus by Alonzo Lewis shows two mills that existed in the Breakheart area. At this time, Water Street, now a main road between Wakefield and Saugus, did not exist. The mill (later called Howlett's Mill) shown in the river bend was used in 1829 to produce wire, but the site had a history dating back to John Gifford's 17th-century ironworks. After its use for manufacturing wire, the mill became a sawmill, followed by a snuff-grinding operation. The photograph below shows a dam in eastern Breakheart that provided power to a linen mill. The Linen and Duck Manufactory Company of Boston was established beside the Newburyport Turnpike in 1814 to produce sail duck for boats. The mill went out of business after the War of 1812 as demand for sail duck declined and cheaper cloth became available. (Above, courtesy of Lynn Museum and Historical Society; below, authors' collection.)

To all christian people John Gifford of Lyn in the County of
Essex in New England Gent sendeth greeting in our Lord God
everlasting, Know ye that the said John Gifford, for in Con
sideration of the sum of two hundred pounds sterling to him in
hand, before the sealing and delivery hereof of well and truly paid by
Capt Tho: Breedon of Boston in the County of Suffolk in New of

This October 1662 deed shows that John Gifford paid 200 pounds sterling to Capt. Thomas Breedon of Boston for 260 acres along the Saugus River, extending west to Reading (now Wakefield). Gifford operated an ironworks on the river until King Philip's War broke out in 1675. In 1700, seven years after Gifford's death, his daughter Margaret Cogswell sold 73 acres of the land, including the mill site, to Timothy Wiley of Reading and Thomas Hawkes of Lynn for 65 pounds. Gifford's ironworks probably looked similar to the one shown in the photograph below, taken at the Saugus Iron Works National Historic Site. (Above, courtesy of Southern Essex Registry of Deeds; below, authors' collection.)

Charles Overly was commissioned in the 1950s to draw this sketch of the 17th-century hammer mill at the Saugus Iron Works. John Gifford's ironworks two miles upstream (on the east side of present-day Breakheart) was probably a similar, but smaller, version of the Saugus Iron Works and would have had a hammer mill much like this. (Courtesy of National Park Service, Saugus Iron Works National Historic Site.)

Know all Men by these Presents, That *I*

William Parker of Saugus in the County of Essex and Common-wealth of Massachusetts, yeoman —.

in consideration of *Eight hundred Dollars —,*
to *me* paid by *John Howlet of Saugus in s.d County Snuff-Manufacturer. —*

the receipt whereof *I do* hereby acknowledge, *have* ~~grant~~, remise*d*, release*d*, and forever **QUIT-CLAIMED,** and *do for myself & my heirs by these presents, remise release & forever quit claim unto the said John Howlet, his —*
heirs and assigns, *All my right, title, interest and estate in & to three fifteenth parts of all that certain real estate, messuages, waters, rights, rights of flowage, build-ings & out houses, rights, privileges & appurtenances to the same belonging to the Lynn wire Manufacturing Company, being the same premises which were originally con-veyed by Samuel Sweetser to David Pratt & others by Deed Recorded in Essex Registry Book 201. Leaf 239 & by David Pratt & others to s.d Lynn Wire Manufacturing Company by Deed Recorded in s.d Registry Book 204 leaf 69, & by Deed from Benjamin Wilson to s.d Lynn Wire Manufactur-*

About 140 years after Gifford's ironworks closed, the site supported a mill for a manufacturing wire. John Howlett bought the mill in 1836 for $800; this deed records the sale. For the next 30 years, Howlett used the mill to grind tobacco into a soft, moist, English-style snuff called Rappee. (Courtesy of Essex County Registry of Deeds.)

Saugus. Mass.
Old Mill.

This c. 1900 postcard shows Howlett's Mill as seen from Water Street in Saugus. On the left is a bridge over the Saugus River, the stone abutments of which (see page 30) may date back to the 1660s when the site was operated as an ironworks. Trolley tracks, which existed between Wakefield and Saugus from about 1890 to 1926, are visible at lower left. On the far right is a dairy farm owned by Byron Hone. In 1900, Howlett's Mill was a sawmill. However, the Lynn Water Board was interested in water rights to the Saugus River. In 1883 and 1884, the board built a canal connecting the milldam to Birch Pond, one of the city reservoirs. In 1888, the City of Lynn bought the mill, dam, and all water rights from Byron Hone for $5,000. The canal was abandoned about 10 years later, when it was replaced by a diversion canal farther upstream. (Courtesy of Saugus Historical Society.)

Young Alice Hone, daughter of Byron S. Hone, pulls a wagon across the bridge beside Howlett's Mill about 1897. Her father owned over 200 acres of farmland in the area. After Hone died in 1925, Alice Hone Bloch and her sister Eva Collins sold the property to Seth C. Sperry for $4,000. Sperry, a golf course developer from Melrose, built the Cedar Glen Golf Club and served as its first manager. (Courtesy of Saugus Public Library.)

This c. 1905 photograph shows water from the Saugus River flowing through the sluiceway of Howlett's Mill dam. Although the timber dam is now gone, the stone abutments still exist. When the dam was later breached, the upstream pond, which had covered several acres, reverted to a stream. (Courtesy of Saugus Historical Society.)

This photograph of a lone fisherman at Howlett's Mill was taken after 1902, when the sawmill stopped operating. In this image, windows at all levels of the mill building are broken. The low water reveals boulders scattered on the river bottom. (Courtesy of Lynn Museum and Historical Society.)

This c. 1905 view of Howlett's Mill looking north shows the Old Highway (with a gate) that was laid out about 1763. The road ran from the mill south to Breakheart Hill Farm on Forest Street (now the Saugus entrance to Breakheart). Until the 1930s, this road was the only road through the Breakheart Hill Forest. (Courtesy of Lynn Museum and Historical Society.)

This photograph labeled "Old Grist Mill" is actually Howlett's Mill (then a sawmill) as viewed from the downstream side of the Saugus River not long before it collapsed in 1907. This image shows the raceway beneath the mill through which water flowed to power the sawmill. (Courtesy of Saugus Historical Society.)

These two images show the rapid deterioration of Howlett's Mill. The above photograph was taken in early 1898, and the image below was taken in 1907, a few months before it was destroyed by a violent thunderstorm on June 19, 1907. (Both, courtesy of Saugus Historical Society.)

This c. 1910 postcard claims that the bridge over the Saugus River at Howlett's Mill is the oldest in Massachusetts. In 1662, John Gifford bought the land (then part of Lynn), where he operated an ironworks, which would have included a bridge to his house. The bridge on the postcard may have used Gifford's stone abutments, but the wooden span probably dates to 1814, when the Lynn Wire Manufacturing Company was established. (Authors' collection.)

This photograph shows the remaining stone abutments of the bridge at Howlett's Mill. These may date back to the first bridge built in the 1660s by John Gifford for his ironworks. The stone foundations of the mill dam also still exist but are obscured by dense vegetation. (Authors' collection.)

Three

PRIVATE FOREST AND CRIME OF THE DECADE

From the early to late industrial periods (1775–1915), the area surrounding Breakheart Reservation was sparsely settled farmland with some manufacturing. Despite the Industrial Revolution, most parcels in present-day Breakheart Reservation remained woodland as they passed through generations, mostly in the same families. Landowners included yeoman farmers, cordwainers (shoemakers), gentlemen, and traders, with some parcels owned by women. Most owners lived elsewhere and used the land, if at all, for wood fuel. The only buildings of note were part of two farms at the eastern and southern boundaries of the Six Hundred Acres connected by the "Old Highway," which, until the 1930s, was the only road through the acreage.

By the second half of the 19th century, cities were crowded and polluted, and it was popular for wealthy men to build rustic retreats in wilderness areas. One of these men was Lynn attorney Benjamin Johnson, who was originally from Saugus. Rather than travel to New Hampshire or Maine, Johnson and his associates, Micajah Clough and John Bartlett, decided to develop their hunting retreat, which they called Breakheart Hill Forest, in the nearby Six Hundred Acres. Beginning in 1891, they set about buying woodlots and farms, including Artemas Edmands's farm. They created two lakes, Upper Pond and Lower Pond, by damming two marshes and stocked them with fish.

In 1897, Johnson and his partners hired George E. Bailey to be caretaker of the farm and forest. Bailey arrived with a woman whom he falsely claimed to be his wife and hired another man, John Best, to help with farming. On the evening of October 8, 1900, after disputes about wages and Best's drinking, Best shot Bailey in the back as Bailey emerged from the barn after a milk run to Saugus. Best dismembered Bailey's body with a knife and axe, then put the pieces into burlap bags, which he dumped into Floating Bridge Pond in Lynn. The crime unraveled rapidly, and Breakheart Hill Farm was headline news for months. After a sensational court trial, Best was found guilty and was electrocuted at Charlestown State Prison. A few years later, the case had faded from memory, and Breakheart Hill Forest was again a quiet refuge from city life.

Benjamin Newhall Johnson (1856–1932) was a prominent attorney and a founder of the Lynn Historical Society. He had a primary role in transforming the Six Hundred Acres into Breakheart Hill Forest, a hunting retreat for his friends and business associates. The 1930 photograph below shows Micajah Pratt Clough (1848–1933) and Harriett Clough on their golden wedding anniversary. Clough was a banker and president of the Lynn Gas and Electric Company and a co-owner of Breakheart Hill Forest. As reported by the *Lynn Daily Item*, "His influence, wisdom and valuable counsel . . . exerted tremendous power for the common good of Lynn. His great hobby was Breakheart Farm in Saugus. . . . It was always maintained, as it is today, true to nature's handiwork on the countryside." (Left, courtesy of Lynn Museum and Historical Society; below, courtesy of Edward Patterson Jr.)

Nathan Mortimer Hawkes (1843–1919) was a prominent lawyer and historian and longtime member of the Lynn Historical Society. He was a representative in the General Court, a state senator, and chairman of the Lynn Board of Park Commissioners. His essay "Semi-historical Rambles Among the Eighteenth-Century Places Along the Saugus River" gives a remarkably detailed description of the Saugus River, including a stretch through Breakheart Reservation. (Courtesy of Lynn Museum and Historical Society.)

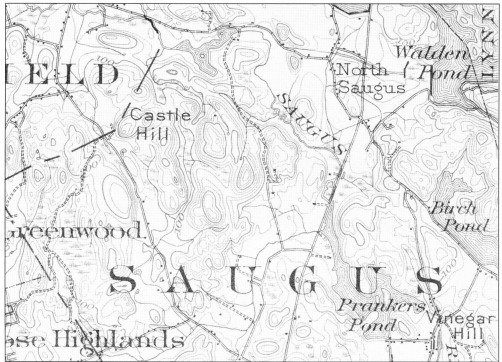

This 1903 topographic map, based on 1898 fieldwork, shows Breakheart Hill Forest before Upper and Lower Ponds were created. It also shows Castle Hill, the area's highest peak, which the White sisters of Wakefield donated to the Breakheart Hill Forestry in 1913. The dashed line is the "Old Highway," connecting Howlett's Mill to Forest Street. Elevation contours are drawn at 20-foot intervals. (Courtesy of Dimond Library, University of New Hampshire.)

Know all men by these Presents that I, Edward W. Edmands, of Saugus, in the County of Essex and Commonwealth of Massachusetts, in consideration of one dollar and other valuable considerations to me paid by Micajah P. Clough, John S. Bartlett, and Benjamin N. Johnson, all of Lynn, in said County of Essex, the receipt thereof is hereby acknowledged, do hereby give, grant, bargain, sell and convey unto the said Micajah P. Clough John S. Bartlett, and Benjamin N. Johnson, a certain lot of land with the buildings thereon, situated in that part of Saugus called Oakdale, at the terminus of Forest Street, so called, and bounded Northerly by the Second Range line of the Six hundred (600) acres, Easterly and Southerly by lands now or late of Dot? Lands, and westerly by the highway, containing about eighteen (18) acres more or less, said premises being sub ... et to mortgage to Charles W. Readdin, guardian of Chas

This 1892 deed records the sale of the 18-acre Edmands' Farm by Edward Edmands (Artemas Edmands's grandson) to Micajah Clough, John Bartlett, and Benjamin Johnson of Lynn for $1. Clough and his associates assumed the mortgage and hired a caretaker, George Parrott, to farm the land and keep hunters and other trespassers out of the forest. (Courtesy of South Essex Registry of Deeds.)

These photographs, taken in 1915 (above) and 1935 (below), show the gate and warning sign that marked the entrance to Breakheart Hill Forest: "This Passageway is Private Property—No Passing Through." At John Best's 1901 trial, Micajah Clough told the court that the gate was built in the spring of 1896 to keep hunters out. Before that, anyone could travel the "Old Highway" into Breakheart to hunt, harvest wood, or travel between Wakefield and North Saugus. (Above, courtesy of Judith Loubris McCarthy; below, courtesy of DCR Archives.)

These 1935 images taken by the MDC soon after the state purchased Breakheart Hill Forest show the earthen dam that Benjamin Johnson and his partners installed in the 1890s and the pond that it created, which they called Upper Pond. The partners built a second dam to create Lower Pond. The dams were rebuilt by the CCC in 1937. In the early 1960s, Upper Pond (also called Sauwake Lake) was renamed Silver Lake after John Leo Silver, a dentist in Saugus, and Lower Pond (also called Wakesau Lake) was renamed Pearce Lake after John A.W. Pearce, principal of Saugus High School. (Both, courtesy of DCR Archives.)

These 1935 photographs of Lower Pond, and those on the next page, show scenes that are virtually unchanged from today. In 1901, 1902, and 1913, Benjamin Johnson stocked the pond with rainbow trout and smallmouth bass. Today, Pearce and Silver Lakes remain relatively unpolluted and support a variety of fish, including bass, pickerel, trout, and musky, as well as painted and snapping turtles. (Both, courtesy of DCR Archives.)

These MDC photographs were both taken from the eastern shore of Lower Pond. In the above image, Crow Hill (elevation 272 feet) is visible in the distance. The image below shows Eagle Rock (elevation 206 feet) near the shore. Eagle Rock is a popular climb to view Boston and the surrounding countryside. (Both, courtesy of DCR Archives.)

Benjamin Johnson, Micajah Clough, and John Bartlett built Breakheart Hill Camp as a hunting lodge and forest refuge for family and friends. The photograph above shows the lodge in 1942, before it was demolished by the MDC sometime between 1945 and 1950. The lodge foundations and the rhododendron garden can still be seen along the Lodge Trail. The photograph below, taken by George Bliss in 1900, shows the interior of Breakheart Hill Camp. In 1939, the MDC allowed Girl Scouts to listen to ghost stories and stay overnight in the lodge. Objects in the lodge include photographs, a canoe, flintlock muskets and pistols, and swords. (Above, courtesy of DCR Archives; below, courtesy of Lynn Museum and Historical Society.)

During an outing on October 28, 1898, George Bliss asked prominent members of the Lynn Historical Society to pose for this photograph in front of Breakheart Hill Camp. Most of these men are identified in the caption for the book cover. The two that are not identified on the cover (on left side of the image) are Philip Augustus Chase and John Clarkson Houghton (facing forward with white beard). (Courtesy of Edward Patterson Jr.)

George Spencer Bliss (1866–1956) was born in Troy, New York. However, both of his parents hailed from Northampton, Massachusetts, with roots going back to the 17th century. After an enlistment in the US Army, he spent most of his life in Lynn, where he worked as an electrical engineer for General Electric and as chief photographer of the Lynn Historical Society. (Courtesy of Edward Patterson Jr.)

These 1935 MDC photographs show Johnson's log cabin located on the east side of Lower Pond, which afforded views of Eagle Rock on the opposite shore. In the photograph below, a canoe is visible in the boathouse below the cabin. The MDC razed the log cabin in 1938. (Both, courtesy of DCR Archives.)

On October 18, 1900, the *Lynn Daily Item* published this sketch of murder victim George E. Bailey. A tall, genial man, Bailey was a familiar face in Wakefield and Saugus where he sold milk and eggs from Breakheart Hill Farm. Originally from Whitefield, Maine, Bailey became the farm's caretaker in October 1897. (Courtesy of Lynn Public Library.)

This sketch of John C. Best was published in the *Lynn Daily Item* on October 22, 1900. He came from Sackville, New Brunswick, and was 38 years old when he murdered fellow farmworker George Bailey and dumped his body in Floating Bridge Pond. Newspapers called the murder the "Crime of the Decade." (Courtesy of Lynn Public Library.)

This 1935 photograph shows the 1771 Breakheart Hill Farmhouse where George Bailey lived with Susie Young and where their son Franklin was born. Bailey had falsely told Johnson and his partners that he and Young were married. Bailey and Young slept downstairs at the back of the house, while John Best, Bailey's hired farmhand, slept in the upstairs bedroom on the left. (Courtesy of DCR Archives.)

At 9:35 p.m. on October 8, 1900, John Best shot George Bailey twice in the back as Bailey came out of the barn's basement door (right side of photograph) after completing a milk run to Saugus. Best used an axe and knife to dismember Bailey's body. He then put the pieces into burlap bags, loaded the bags onto a wagon, and drove six miles to Floating Bridge Pond in Lynn. (Courtesy of DCR Archives.)

On October 17, 1900, the *Lynn Daily Item* ran these sensational headlines. That morning, two men passing by Floating Bridge Pond had discovered a floating burlap bag containing the headless, armless, and legless torso of a large man. Police immediately set about finding the remaining body parts as well as the murderer. (Courtesy of Lynn Public Library.)

This 1898 photograph shows Floating Bridge Pond in eastern Lynn where John Best disposed of Bailey's body. The 500-foot-long wooden bridge was built in 1804 across Collins Pond as part of the Salem Turnpike, the main highway from Boston to Salem. The floating design was used because the pond was too wide for most bridge spans of the time, and the pond was rumored to be bottomless. (Courtesy of Lynn Museum and Historical Society.)

This view of the Floating Bridge in Lynn shows foot, wagon, and cow traffic less than a year after Bailey's remains had been recovered. Travelers on heavy wagons proceeded cautiously as the weight would sometimes sink the bridge deck to the level of the water. (Courtesy of Lynn Museum and Historical Society.)

On October 18, 1900, the day after Bailey's body was discovered in Floating Bridge Pond, the *Lynn Daily Item* published this sketch of Breakheart Hill Farm, the scene of the crime. A month later, police returned to the pond to search for the axe used to commit the murder. Instead, they discovered the body of another man, Robert J. Burns of Lynn, who had apparently committed suicide. (Courtesy of Lynn Public Library.)

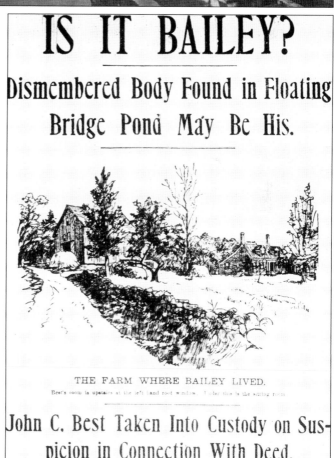

IS IT BAILEY?

Dismembered Body Found in Floating Bridge Pond May Be His.

THE FARM WHERE BAILEY LIVED.

Best's room is upstairs at the left hand roof window. Under this is the sitting room

John C. Best Taken Into Custody on Suspicion in Connection With Deed.

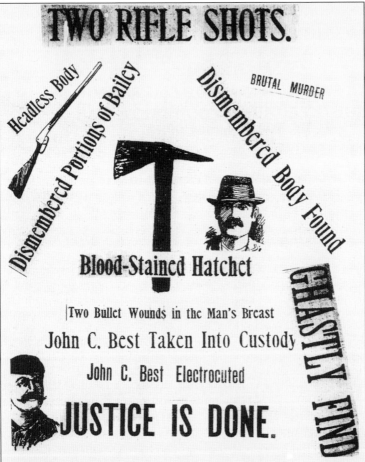

TWO RIFLE SHOTS.

Headless Body

Dismembered Portions of Bailey

BRUTAL MURDER

Dismembered Body Found

Blood-Stained Hatchet

GHASTLY FIND

Two Bullet Wounds in the Man's Breast

John C. Best Taken Into Custody

John C. Best Electrocuted

JUSTICE IS DONE.

The Bailey murder was front-page news in the *Lynn Daily Item* for 23 consecutive days in October and November 1900. On October 22, the *Item* illustrated the crowds of people visiting the farm (above). The *Item* captivated their readers with a steady flow of sensational headlines until the end came on September 9, 1902, at 12:27 a.m. when John Best was electrocuted at Charlestown State Prison nearly two years after the murder. According to the *Lynn Daily Item*, he helped the guards with strapping himself in the electric chair and remained "cool and stolid to the last." (Both, courtesy of Lynn Public Library.)

After the sensation of the murder passed, Breakheart Hill Forest was again a refuge from the city. This photograph, taken on a sunny day in late March 1907, captures a scene of the Clough family playing bridge on the porch of the Breakheart Hill Camp. (Courtesy of Edward Patterson Jr.)

Micajah Clough (far right) and his family pose at the Breakheart Hill Camp in late March 1907. The Cloughs lived on Ocean Street in Lynn for many years and had eight children. (Courtesy of Edward Patterson Jr.)

Young members of the Clough family found creative ways to amuse themselves at Breakheart Hill Camp. In March 1907, a photographer was on hand to capture this macabre prank, which would have made quite an impression on any unsuspecting visitor. (Courtesy of Edward Patterson Jr.)

During a March 1907 visit to Breakheart Hill Camp, one of the Clough boys dressed like Pancho Villa and posed for a photograph with old weapons borrowed from their normal perch above the fireplace in the lodge. (Courtesy of Edward Patterson Jr.)

Looking neat but uncomfortable in starched white shirts and ties, two Clough boys gaze out a window in the Breakheart Hill Camp in March 1907. Undoubtedly, the boys are looking forward to getting back to their main activities of fishing, swimming, and exploring the woods. (Courtesy of Edward Patterson Jr.)

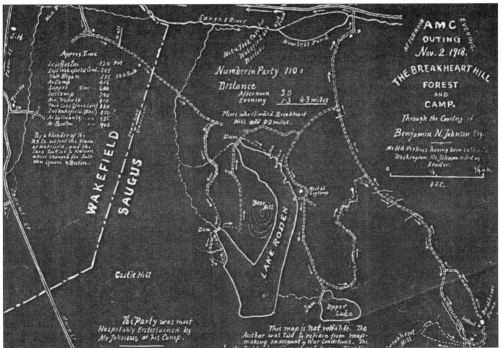

This rough map shows the route for a November 2, 1918, outing to the forest by the Appalachian Mountain Club. After arriving from Boston by train, 110 club members hiked along trails before enjoying a meal prepared by Benjamin Johnson. On this map, Lower Pond is called Lake Roden and Eagle Rock is called Bear Hill, and a disclaimer states: "This map is not reliable . . . on account of War Conditions." (Courtesy of Lynn Museum and Historical Society.)

Know all men by these presents that whereas, Nancy White, late of Wakefield in the County of Middlesex and Commonwealth of Massachusetts, by her last will, duly allowed by the Probate Court of said County, provided that about nine (9) acres of land in Saugus, adjoining the Town of Wakefield included in which is Castle Hill, should be devoted forever as a place to be kept open for the benefit of the people of said Town and the public generally, and devised her interest in said lands to her executors in trust for that purpose, and directed her said executors to use whatever means seemed best to accomplish it, and authorized them to convey the same to the State or any Town or Corporation to accomplish best this purpose, and

On September 24, 1913, Mary Eaton Aborn sold nine acres of land that included Castle Hill in Saugus to Breakheart Hill Forestry, thus fulfilling her late sister Nancy White's wishes that the land be preserved "as a place to be kept open for the benefit of the people . . . and the public generally." The sisters had offered to sell the land to the state but were turned down. The 1834 map (below) drawn for their father, John White Jr., shows the parcel's location east of the Wakefield-Saugus town line and northeast of Main Street. Surveyors in those days used rods and links to measure distances. A rod is 16.5 feet, and a link is about eight inches. (Both, courtesy of the Southern Essex Registry of Deeds.)

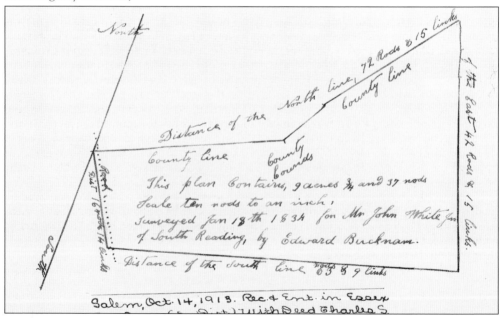

Four

Breakheart Hill Farm and the Parkers

Breakheart Hill Farm, the site of Bailey's murder, had a history dating back to the late 18th century. The 18-acre farm was located between the first and second range lines of the eight range lines that defined the Six Hundred Acres. This land was first owned by Daniel Hitchings, followed by his son Nathan, who built the farmhouse in 1771 and fought in the Revolutionary War four years later. In 1830, Nathan's son Benjamin sold the farm to Thomas Houghton for $375, who, four years later, sold it to Artemas Edmands for $400. The deed describes it as "a certain farm lying in Saugus, containing eighteen acres, be the same more or less, bounded as follows, viz. Westerly on a road leading from the house of Ira Draper to the house of William Edmands [Artemas's uncle], westerly on heirs of Sarah Hitchings and heirs of Haven Hawkes, easterly and southerly on land formerly owned by Caroline Plummer and sold by her to Lot Edmands [Artemas's father], or however otherwise bounded with all the buildings thereon." Artemas Edmands and his family owned the farm for over 40 years. In 1892, his grandson, Edward Edmands, sold the farm to Breakheart Hill Forestry for $1. Benjamin Johnson and his associates assumed the mortgage and hired a caretaker, George Parrott, to farm the land and keep hunters and other trespassers out of the forest. George Bailey replaced Parrott as caretaker in 1897. In 1901, after Bailey was murdered by John Best (see chapter 3), George Parker of Saugus became caretaker and lived with his family on the farm until his death in 1923.

The early 20th century was a time when more than half of the nation's population lived on small farms similar to Breakheart Hill Farm. These farms were labor intensive, and many farmers, like the Parkers, still relied on animal power. The daily lives of the Parkers give a glimpse back to a romanticized time in American history, a time when families worked together and patterned their lives on the cycle of seasons.

Know all Men by these Presents, That I,

Thomas Houghton of Saugus in the County of Essex & Commonwealth of Massachusetts, Yeoman,

in consideration of *four hundred dollars*
to *me* paid by *Artemas Edmands of said*

Saugus, Cordwainer,

the receipt whereof *is* hereby acknowledged, *do by these presents,* grant, remise, release, and forever QUIT-CLAIM, unto the said *Artemas, his*

heirs and assigns,
all the right, title, interest and estate in and to a certain farm lying in Saugus, containing eighteen acres, be the same more or less, bounded as follows, viz. Westerly on a road leading from the house of Ira Draper to the house of William Edmands, Westerly on heirs of Sarah Hitchins and heirs of Haven Hawks, Easterly and Southerly on land formerly owned by Caroline Plummer, and sold by her to Lot Edmands, or however otherwise bounded, with all the buildings thereon.

To Have and to Hold, the *above released* premises,

to *him* the said *Artemas*
his heirs and assigns, *to his & their use & behoof* forever:
so that neither *I* the said *Thomas*
nor *my* heirs, or any other person or persons
claiming *by*, from or under *me* or them, or in the name, right, or stead of *me* or them, shall or will, by any way or means, have, claim, or demand any right or title to the *above released* premises, or to any part or parcel thereof, forever. *In Witness Whereof, I the said Thomas and Sarah his wife in token of relinquishing her right of dower in the premises*

have hereunto set *our* hands and seals this *first* day of *April* in the year of our Lord one thousand eight hundred and *thirty four*

This deed documents the sale of Breakheart Hill Farm in April 1834 to Artemas Edmands (aged 21) from Thomas Houghton for $400. Four months later, Edmands married Margarate Wilson. Artemas had four children and worked on the 18-acre farm for 41 years. Saugus town records show that, in 1850, the Edmands had one horse, two cows, and two pigs and that the farm yielded 40 bushels of corn and 120 bushels of potatoes. (Courtesy of Southern Essex Registry of Deeds.)

The gravesite of Nathan Hitchings (1741–1821) and his wife, Abigail (Larrabee) Hitchings (1737–1819), is located in the Old Burial Ground in Saugus. In 1771, the same year he was married, Hitchings built a farm on land that was part of the 1706 Six Hundred Acres. Four years later, after the Battles of Lexington and Concord, he joined the Continental Army and fought for six years. (Authors' collection.)

George Bliss took this photograph of the house at Breakheart Hill Farm in 1913 when caretaker George Parker lived there with his family. Parker was hired by Benjamin Johnson and his partners after the previous caretaker, George Bailey, was murdered. Before becoming part of Breakheart Hill Forestry, the farm was owned by Artemas Edmands, who sold milk, eggs, and apples in Saugus. (Courtesy of DCR Archives.)

These c. 1915 photographs show views from two directions. The above photograph shows the Breakheart Hill farmhouse from Forest Street near the present-day entrance to Breakheart Reservation. The photograph below shows a view from the farmhouse looking southeast across a meadow that extended to the Newburyport Turnpike (US Route 1). (Both, courtesy of Judith Loubris McCarthy.)

This c. 1915 photograph shows the Breakheart Hill farmhouse, barn, and maintenance shed. The sketch below, published in the *Lynn Daily Item* in October 1900, shows the back of the farmhouse. This Saltbox style, characterized by a long, pitched roof that slopes down to the back, was popular in colonial New England. Note the well and the wooden boardwalk from the house to the barn that helped to keep shoes from getting muddy or wet. (Above, courtesy of Judith Loubris McCarthy; below, courtesy of Lynn Public Library.)

This c. 1915 photograph shows George Wallace Parker (1857–1923), who became caretaker of Breakheart Hill Farm after George Bailey was murdered in 1900. Parker was a direct descendant of colonial immigrant John Parker of Wiltshire, England. In 1884, he married Lucinda Bowley Jackson of Lynn (1858–1945) (below). Of their nine children, six survived infancy: Charles, Bertha, William, Frank "Ernest," Octavia "Tav," and Jane Elizabeth "Bess." Before moving to the farm, George worked as a milkman and railroad laborer. Their last child, Bess, was born at Breakheart Hill Farm in 1901. In 1915, Lucinda suffered a stroke, which paralyzed her left arm. After 1935, she moved to Wakefield, Massachusetts, to live with her daughter Octavia and Octavia's husband, Roland Oliver, a bank teller. (Both, courtesy of Judith Loubris McCarthy.)

Like many farms, Breakheart Hill Farm had an apple orchard. This was located south of the farmhouse and was destroyed in 1935 to make way for a CCC camp. Apples had been a popular farm product since colonial times, as they stored well and had many uses. For centuries, women both baked and brewed apples, producing apple butter and apple pie for eating and cider for drinking. At right, Ernest Parker is pruning an apple tree on the farm. These apples were Baldwin apples, which were named after Col. Loammi Baldwin (1745–1807), an engineer and builder of the Middlesex Canal and a soldier in the Revolutionary War. This apple was first identified on a farm in nearby Wilmington about 1750 and promoted by Colonel Baldwin after 1784. (Both, courtesy of Judith Loubris McCarthy.)

The above photograph shows a teenaged Bess Parker about 1917 driving a carriage drawn by Prince, the family's favorite horse. Her mother, Lucinda, sits in the rear holding their dog Peggy. Below, Bess helps older brother Ernest with spring plowing. Oddly, both are wearing suit jackets with starched shirts and ties, and Bess's suit is protected with overalls. (Both, courtesy of Judith Loubris McCarthy.)

These photographs show Ernest Parker cutting hay with a sickle mower drawn by Prince. This mower, invented by Cyrus McCormick and associates in the 1840s, was still in common use in New England in the early 20th century. Breakheart Hill Farm, like many small farms in New England, was located on hilly and rocky terrain and had a short growing season. Therefore, the Parkers, like other farmers in the area, took advantage of the good grazing season and focused on livestock, especially dairy, and growing hay. (Both, courtesy of Judith Loubris McCarthy.)

Brothers Charles and Ernest Parker (wearing the bow tie) head out to collect another load of hay. The family owned four horses, two white and two black. Three names are known: Prince, Daisy, and Sam. The Parkers often discussed their horses and treated them like members of the family. (Courtesy of Judith Loubris McCarthy.)

Bess Parker uses a hay rake pulled by Prince. These rakes would pull and gather dry hay into windrows, which are rows of cut hay left to dry in a field before being bundled and taken to a barn. (Courtesy of Judith Loubris McCarthy.)

Bess Parker smiles and older brother William playfully holds a puppy while sitting atop a hay wagon in front of the barn at Breakheart Hill Farm. Hay dried in the field and, in late summer, was brought to the barn and stored in the hayloft. (Courtesy of Judith Loubris McCarthy.)

L. Newhall captured this photograph of two snowshoers in Breakheart Hill Forest during the winter in 1910. With the redesign of snowshoes using lightweight materials, this sport has recently become popular in Breakheart. (Courtesy of Lynn Museum and Historical Society.)

This 1910 photograph of a long woodpile in the snow is credited to L. Newhall and may have been taken near the old Wiley Street entrance to Breakheart. For many years, this was the most popular entrance to the reservation for Wakefield residents. It was replaced after 1953 by a new entrance near Wakefield High School. (Courtesy of Lynn Museum and Historical Society.)

Bess Parker had frequently been unwell as a child, and the family doctor recommended that she spend as much time as possible outdoors. This suited her, and many photographs show her engaged in outdoor activities. This c. 1917 photograph shows her skiing in the apple orchard. Skiing was a relatively new sport, and her skis may have been made from barrel staves, although some skis were available in local shops. (Courtesy of Judith Loubris McCarthy.)

This c. 1917 photograph shows Bess Parker preparing to ski down a gentle slope at Breakheart Hill Farm. This slope led to open fields that in 1935, along with the apple orchard, became the location of a CCC camp (see page 80). (Courtesy of Judith Loubris McCarthy.)

This c. 1920 photograph shows Lucinda Parker (granddaughter of George and Lucinda) on her white horse. At this time, the young Lucinda lived on Water Street in Saugus with her parents, William and Lena Parker, and her aunt and uncle, Tav (Parker) and Roland Oliver. (Courtesy of Judith Loubris McCarthy.)

Prince stands ready to pull a sled while his rider photographs this wintery scene at Breakheart Hill Forest. Telephone lines that Johnson and partners had installed before 1900 are visible in the sky in the background. In the early 20th century, horse-drawn sleds were used to pack down snow on roads. Snowplows, if available, were horse-drawn wooden wedge-plows. The first snowplows designed for motor equipment were manufactured in 1913 by Good Roads Machinery in Kennett Square, Pennsylvania. (Courtesy of Judith Loubris McCarthy.)

Bess Parker enjoyed skiing in the Breakheart Hill Forest, which had many trails and bridle paths. Before cars, this was an ideal means of getting around in winter, especially when deep snow blanketed the countryside. In the early 1900s, people also began to recognize the health benefits of skiing. (Courtesy of Judith Loubris McCarthy.)

The c. 1916 photograph captured Bess Parker standing on Prince. Before attempting this feat, she wisely laid folded blankets on the horse's rump. She is wearing a sailor's shirt with knotted kerchief, which had long been a popular clothing style, but usually for young boys. (Courtesy of Judith Loubris McCarthy.)

Tav Parker poses with one of the family's horses inside the Breakheart Hill Farm barn about 1917. (Courtesy of Judith Loubris McCarthy.)

On a chilly, but calm, fall day about 1914, a group of young people, neatly dressed and wearing hats and hair ribbons for a special occasion, gathered for a photograph in front of the barn. Two girls on the right are Adele "Addie" and Florence Edmands, great-grandchildren of Artemas Edmands. They lived on a neighboring farm. (Courtesy of Judith Loubris McCarthy.)

In this 1916 image, 15-year-old Bess Parker poses with Prince next to a boulder at Breakheart Hill Farm. The photographer may have been Bess's older brother Charles. This boulder appears in many photographs and is still present near the Saugus entrance to Breakheart Reservation, although the barn was razed in early 1973. (Courtesy of Judith Loubris McCarthy.)

This c. 1915 photograph shows Winnette "Winnie" Parker (wife of Charles Parker) with her four-year-old son George Adelbert "Dell" on a horse at Breakheart Hill Farm. In 1887, Winnie was born on a farm in Kenduskeag, Maine (just northwest of Bangor), and moved to Charlestown, Massachusetts, as a child. Sometime before 1910, she met Charles Parker at a Temperance meeting in Charlestown. (Courtesy of Judith Loubris McCarthy.)

This c. 1917 photograph shows Ernest Parker and John James Mahoney, who married Bess Parker in 1923, at Breakheart Hill Farm. (Courtesy of Judith Loubris McCarthy.)

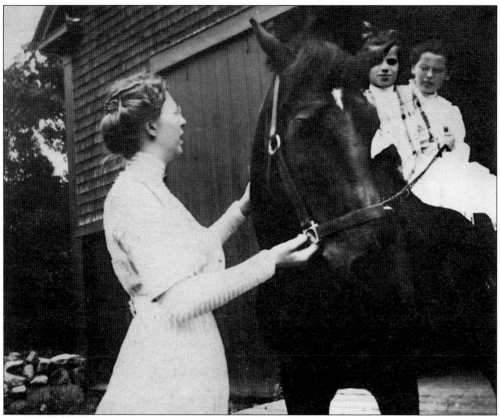

This c. 1915 photograph shows Lena Griffin Parker holding Prince's reins for Bess and Tav (at far right). Lena was married to William Parker and worked as a private nurse. By 1930, she and her family had moved to Lynn where William worked as a foreman for the Lynn Gas and Electric Company. (Courtesy of Judith Loubris McCarthy.)

Addie and Florence Edmands lived on a nearby dairy farm. They were the great-grandchildren of Artemas Edmands, who had owned Breakheart Hill Farm from 1834 to 1875. It was Artemas's grandson Edward (Addie and Florence's uncle) who sold the farm in 1892 to Breakheart Hill Forestry for $1. (Courtesy of Judith Loubris McCarthy.)

Winnie, Tav, and Bess Parker ride on a buckboard, called a democrat wagon, to the Breakheart Hill Farm. The man in the back of the wagon appears to be Benjamin Johnson, one of the owners of the farm and Breakheart Hill Forest. (Courtesy of Judith Loubris McCarthy.)

Tav and her husband, Roland "Rollie" Oliver (1899–1980) were just 19 and 18, respectively, when they married in 1917. In 1920, they lived with William Parker and his family on Water Street in Saugus, and Rollie worked as a bank teller. Ten years and two daughters later, they moved to Rollie's hometown of Wakefield, where Tav worked as an underwear sales lady. (Courtesy of Judith Loubris McCarthy.)

Charles and Winnie Parker and their
children, George, Philip, and Helen, enjoy
a picnic lunch at Breakheart Hill Farm.
Winnie is on the right. Lucinda Parker
is behind her son Charles on the left.
(Courtesy of Judith Loubris McCarthy.)

In this c. 1917 photograph, Tav Parker wears
a headband with her hair down for an event
with the Pocahontas Club in Saugus. Tav's
grandfather William O. Jackson (Lucinda's
father) was a Saugus Indian. Tav was not
the only member of the Parker family to
celebrate their Native American heritage.
Tav's brother Charles became head sachem
of the Saugus branch of the Redman's Club.
(Courtesy of Judith Loubris McCarthy.)

Ernest Parker (at right) poses at Breakheart Hill Farm in his World War I Army uniform about 1918. He served as a runner between trenches at the front and also served on the American Expeditionary Force in France and Germany after the war. Below, in a photograph taken the same year, Parker's friend and future brother-in-law John Mahoney shows off his sailor uniform. (Both, courtesy of Judith Loubris McCarthy.)

Adele "Addie" Edmands (1905–1983), great-granddaughter of Artemas Edmands, stands on the porch of the log cabin on the east side of Lower Pond in 1917. She and her younger sister Florence often rode horses and played with the Parker girls. Below, Bess (Parker) and John Mahoney pose on the same porch on their wedding day on April 2, 1923. (Both, courtesy of Judith Loubris McCarthy.)

These photographs show Bess (Parker) and John Mahoney at Breakheart Hill Farm about 1925 (above) and on their diamond anniversary on April 2, 1983. John holds the photograph taken at the log cabin on Lower Pond (Pearce Lake) on their wedding day 60 years earlier (see page 72). (Both, courtesy of Judith Loubris McCarthy.)

In this c. 1915 image, William Parker (left) and John Mahoney pose with Peggy in front of the large boulder next to the barn at Breakheart Hill Farm. Almost 100 years later, their great-niece Judith Loubris McCarthy poses in front of the same boulder. (Authors' collection.)

Five

THE 1930S AND THE CCC

At the turn of the 20th century, Theodore Roosevelt popularized the idea of setting land aside for protection and public use. At this time, two conservation-minded sisters, Nancy White and Mary Eaton Aborn, owned land around Castle Hill, the highest peak in the original Six Hundred Acres. Before she died in 1902, Nancy White requested in her will that "about 9 acres of land in Saugus, adjoining the town of Wakefield included in which is Castle Hill, should be devoted forever as a place to be kept open for the benefit of the people of said town and the public generally." However, the state turned down the donation, and in 1913, Mary Aborn donated it to the Breakheart Hill Forestry. Thus, it appears that the Breakheart Hill Forestry was intended to be used for both acquiring land and for protecting it for the future.

By 1930, Benjamin Johnson and Micajah Clough still owned Breakheart Hill Forest (John Bartlett had died in 1925), but they knew that its time as a private retreat was passing. They also witnessed the contrasting fate of two parcels of land to the east of their forest. In 1929, George Nihan negotiated the purchase of 40 acres of land for a Boy Scout camp. The following year, about 130 acres of farmland northwest of Camp Nihan were sold to golf course developer Seth Sperry. While the forest was largely preserved at Camp Nihan, the woods and farmland to the northwest were extensively altered to create the Cedar Glen Golf Course.

In 1934, executors for Johnson and Clough sold the forest to the Metropolitan District Commission (MDC). The timing coincided with the start of Franklin Roosevelt's Civilian Conservation Corps (CCC) program to employ young men. Within months of the sale, the MDC turned it over to the federal government to set up a CCC camp. Over a six-year period, CCC boys built roads and trails, planted trees, and restored the Upper and Lower Pond dams. Their efforts resulted in the return of wildlife that had become rare, including beavers, fishers, coyotes, blue herons, and owls.

This c. 1950 photograph shows George E. Nihan and his wife, Annie, on Tracy Lane in Lynn, Massachusetts. As scout executive for the Lynn Council Boy Scouts, Nihan negotiated the 1929 purchase of property, which bordered Breakheart Hill Forest on the east, for the Boy Scouts. An August 1929 edition of the *Lynn Daily Item* reported that the camp would be developed "for use by the 40 troops of Boy Scouts in Greater Lynn to augment like work carried on in the summer months by the boys at Camp Powow." (Courtesy of James Nihan.)

Boy Scouts at Camp Nihan line up for lunch in August 1951. The 40-acre camp was dedicated in October 1930 with 500 Boy Scouts present. George Nihan spoke at length about the need for this scouting camp located closer to Lynn and the activities it would offer, including swimming, mapmaking, archery, and outdoor cooking. (Courtesy of Edward Patterson Jr.)

Camp Nihan is located on the Saugus River and the shores of Peckham Pond. The property was bought by the MDC in the early 1970s. In the late 1990s, the MDC's Reservations and Historic Sites Division developed an environmental education center for both girls and boys and allowed the public to reserve overnight stays through ReserveAmerica. com. (Authors' collection.)

The Cedar Glen Golf Club, which bordered Breakheart Hill Forest on the north, occupies land formerly owned by Byron S. Hone, who, like his father Philip, ran a large dairy farm. In November 1930, after Byron died, his daughters Alice Hone Bloch and Eva Collins sold over 130 acres to Seth Sperry of nearby Melrose for $4,000. He developed the land into a nine-hole golf course and was the club's first president. (Authors' collection.)

Reduced Prices **At Newly Improved**

Cedar Glen Golf Club

WELCOME TRANSIENTS

WEEK-DAYS

WEEK DAYS 50c per round, $1.00 All Day

SAT. AFTERNOONS, SUNDAYS, HOLIDAYS
$1.00 round; $2.00 All Day

LADIES 75c SUNDAY and HOLIDAY AFTERNOONS

Located at WATER STREET, NORTH SAUGUS
TEL. SAUGUS 10977

In 1932, this advertisement for the "newly improved" Cedar Glen Golf Club appeared in the *Melrose Free Press*. On weekdays, a day of golf cost $1; on weekends, the price rose to $2. Women were charged a lower price Sundays and holidays; however, it is not clear whether they were permitted to play on other days. Although golf originated in Scotland during the Middle Ages, it was not widely popular in the United States until the late 19th century. At that time, it was generally considered a man's game, partly because women's clothes were restrictive and not conducive to full swings. Women did not gain stature in the golf world until the 1940s, when the Women's Professional Golf Association (WPGA) was founded (1944), replaced by the Ladies Professional Golf Association (LPGA) in 1950. (Courtesy of Cedar Glen Golf Club.)

Landscape architect and MDC consultant Arthur Shurcliff (1870–1957), shown in the photograph at right, proposed "preliminary sketch plans" for Breakheart Reservation in February 1935. Famous for his skill in reinterpreting colonial American landscapes, Shurcliff helped design Old Sturbridge Village, the Charles River Esplanade, Franklin Park Zoo, and Colonial Williamsburg. The sketch shows roads, trails, picnic grounds, and parking spaces throughout Breakheart as well as the proposed CCC camp. In September 1935, Walter Hatch, CCC camp supervisor and landscape designer (specializing in golf courses), approved Shurcliff's design. However, the completed reservation incorporated fewer roads and picnic areas. (Right, courtesy of Massachusetts Historical Society; below, courtesy of DCR Archives.)

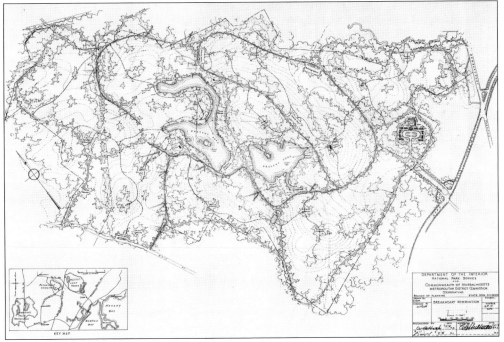

The hay field and orchard at Breakheart Hill Farm are shown here before they were destroyed to build a CCC camp in June 1935. Notice the cows grazing among the apple trees. In the photograph below, by Malcolm "Dyke" Patterson, the Breakheart CCC camp is beginning to take shape. While building the camp, workers slept in Army tents nearby. (Above, courtesy of DCR Archives; below, courtesy of Malcolm Patterson Jr.)

This Spirit of the CCC poster shows an enthusiastic CCC boy standing in front of his barracks with tools of his profession as well as books and a pen, showing that basic reading and writing skills were as valued as physical skills. From 1933 to 1942, the CCC program taught more than 40,000 young men to read. (Courtesy of DCR.)

Work crews are shown erecting the first barracks at the new CCC camp. Twenty men from Vermont and three from Massachusetts (including Malcolm Patterson from Lynn) were transferred from the 167th Company in North Reading and arrived in Saugus in June 1935. The rest of the company, comprised of 167 men from Fort Devens, arrived at Breakheart two months later in August 1935. (Courtesy of Malcolm Patterson Jr.)

Malcolm Patterson took this rooftop view of the barracks of the 1149th Company during the summer of 1935. The metal chimneys are for the potbellied stoves that heated the buildings. Electrical power lines and drinking water mains were extended from the Newburyport Turnpike (US Route 1) to the CCC camp in late August 1935. (Courtesy of Malcolm Patterson Jr.)

On a hot summer day in 1935, three "Vermont Boys" of the 1149th Company arrive at the new CCC barracks with a truckload of mattresses. From left to right are Ralph Ploof of Windsor, Vermont; Red Sawyer of Woodstock, Vermont; and Ben Sanborn of Chelsea, Vermont. (Courtesy of Malcolm Patterson Jr.)

On August 28, 1935, the CCC camp was officially opened. From left to right are (first row) Congressman (later speaker of the House of Representatives) John McCormack, Joseph Casey, Lauretta (McCormick) Bresnahan (state selecting agent for the CCC; known as "Mother of the CCC"), Sen. David Walsh, Col. Harold Hernu, Raymond Estabrook (camp commander), Congressman William Connery Jr. (forestry superintendent), and state representative C.F. Nelson Pratt; (second row) Capt. George Shields and Lieutenant Carlin. (Courtesy of Edward Patterson Jr.)

Malcolm Patterson faced east from Forest Street to capture this image of the CCC barracks in 1937. Trees and scrubs on the landscaped grounds are well established, and fieldstones border the walkways. A magnified view shows a group of men (right center) standing in line. The sign beside the road says, "Automobiles Not Allowed Beyond This Point." (Courtesy of Malcolm Patterson Jr.)

This photograph shows the CCC barracks in the winter of 1937. Lot Edmands's farm is visible in the distance on the right. The farm was demolished in the 1960s to make way for a shopping center along US Route 1. (Courtesy of Malcolm Patterson Jr.)

Each day, about six CCC enrollees cooked and served three meals a day in this mess hall, although many men took bagged lunches containing two sandwiches (peanut butter and jelly the most popular) and fruit to their project sites. The *Wakefield Daily Item* reported that the average CCC boy gained 25 pounds. In 1987, Vincent Piccole of Lynn said, "I used to come home once a week with pork chops. What a delicacy that was! In six months, I grew six inches and put on 40 pounds." (Courtesy of DCR.)

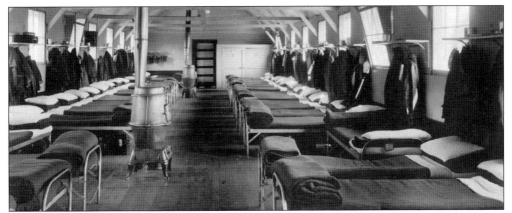

This 1937 photograph shows the military-style living quarters for the CCC men. The emphasis placed on discipline is revealed in this unadorned, meticulously ordered room. Even with three wood stoves, the men needed heavy woolen blankets to keep warm in the poorly insulated barracks. A magnified view shows buckets on the back wall for use in case of fire. (Courtesy of DCR.)

Educational programs at the camps emphasized literacy as well as job training. This 1937 photograph shows that the men had access to a well-stocked camp library. In September 1935, Michael J. Curran became the camp's educational advisor. He hired four teachers and also arranged to have CCC students take night classes at Lynn Classical and Malden High Schools. (Courtesy of DCR.)

Each enrollee was issued a booklet of canteen coupons worth 25¢ each. Expenditures at the canteen were deducted from pay. This photograph shows items for sale, including Coca-Cola, Camel cigarettes, Union Leader tobacco, Phillies cigars, Juicy Fruit gum, Nestle's Crunch, Kraft caramels, Bolster (now Clark) bars, Oh Henry!, Butterfinger, Colgate and Palmolive toothpaste, and Ivory soap. Most things cost 5¢. (Courtesy of DCR.)

This 1937 CCC patch belonged to Russell S. Everett of Lynn, Massachusetts. This was probably bought at the canteen, which sold souvenirs such as pins and pocketknives with the CCC logo. In 1987, Everett told a reporter for the *Lynn Daily Item* that "I was a macho kind of kid. I was extremely healthy. . . . I weighed 117 pounds. . . . In my first 30 days at the camp I put on 15 pounds." (Courtesy of Edward Patterson Jr.)

Even matchbooks were inscribed with the CCC logo and company number, like this one from 1935. Modeled after the military, CCC boys began each day with reveille, slept in military barracks, ate in a mess hall, wore surplus World War I clothes, and had their records maintained by the War Department. (Courtesy of DCR.)

In winter 1936, Malcolm Patterson took this photograph of the camp woodshop (center) and the motor pool garage, which was equipped with 10 bays. The woodshop was located in the present-day parking area in front of the Breakheart visitor center. (Courtesy of Malcolm Patterson Jr.)

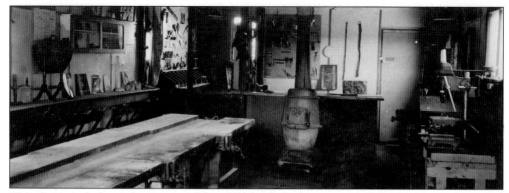

This photograph shows the interior of the woodshop, which was a part of the CCC camp from 1935 to 1941. This well-equipped shop was constructed by combining four portable buildings. Similar to other CCC camps, the Breakheart camp offered training in woodworking and blacksmithing. (Courtesy of DCR.)

Personnel files were kept in this neat office at the CCC camp. This was also where paperwork was done (note two typewriters on desks). The annual cost for each enrollee for food, clothing, overhead, and allotments to dependents was about $1,000. CCC enrollee records are now at the National Personnel Records Center (NPRC) of the National Archives. (Courtesy of DCR.)

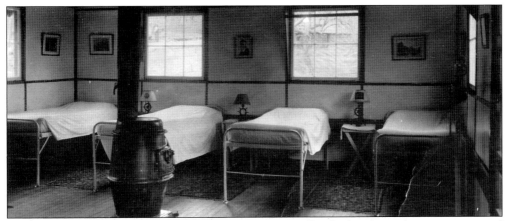

This photograph shows the camp infirmary. Every enrollee had a physical examination and inoculations. For many enrollees, the CCC provided their first encounter with professional health care. At Breakheart, the camp physician was Dr. Alexander MacRobbie of Lynn, Massachusetts. At each camp, one or more CCC enrollees were trained in first aid. (Courtesy of DCR.)

The greatest threat to parks is forest fires. As soon as the CCC camp opened, enrollees began building firebreaks and fire ponds and removing deadwood. In August 1935, Breakheart CCC men worked with firefighters to put out a 10-acre fire near Cedar Glen Golf Course. This photograph shows, from left to right, three Vermont boys, Benny Sanborn, Albert Brooks, and Ted Sawyer. The truck has a pump for water. Looking on at right is camp commander Lt. John J. Shields. (Courtesy of Malcolm Patterson Jr.)

A CCC work crew from 1936 poses in front of the barn at Breakheart Hill Farm, which was used to store maintenance vehicles. The men are, roughly from left to right, Drinkwater, Dee, Munis, Malcolm Patterson, Smitty, Bob Taylor, Barns, McFarland, Joe Urban, Oley, Bill Travers, Phillips, Duke Harrison, Bud Johnson, and Charlie Guest. (Courtesy of Malcolm Patterson Jr.)

CCC boys relax during a work detail outside of Breakheart, possibly in nearby Lawrence. During March and April 1936, CCC boys from Breakheart participated in emergency response and disaster relief actions after record floods affected that city. (Courtesy of Malcolm Patterson Jr.)

Although the young men in the CCC worked hard, there was still time for fun. They swam (as shown here), fished, ice skated, and played baseball and basketball with the Saugus Twilight and Eastern Sub-District CCC leagues. The men are, from left to right, (first row) Pop Leach, Doc Jones, and Lynn Morgan; (second row) Austin Johnson, Charlie LeMarsh, Wilbur King, Everett Drown, Ralph Ploof, and Red Sawyer. (Courtesy of Malcolm Patterson Jr.)

Malcolm Patterson captured this image of a group of CCC enrollees, some dressed in suits and ties, beside one of the barracks. Joe Folks, one of only a few African Americans working in the camp, is standing on the left. Ralph Ploof and Doc Jones are kneeling on the right. (Courtesy of Malcolm Patterson Jr.)

CCC men take a break from shoveling snow in the winter of 1935 to line up for a photograph by Malcolm Patterson. From their casual stances and spirit of play, it is evident that the men had developed camaraderie from living and working together. (Courtesy of Malcolm Patterson Jr.)

Two Vermont boys of strikingly different appearance, Jack Rider (left) and Charlie LeMarsh, pause while cleaning up after camping at Breakheart Hill Farm. The Vermont boys lived in Army tents in the orchard in 1935 while they constructed the camp buildings and Parcher baseball field. Parcher Field, which still exists, was named after George C. Parcher, a Saugus physician who was a major in World War 1 and the first commander of Saugus American Legion Post 210. (Courtesy of Malcolm Patterson Jr.)

Good friends, Malcolm "Dyke" Patterson (left) and Bill Travers, sit on field stones surrounding the flagpole at the CCC camp in 1936. Two barracks are visible in the background. When the CCC camp was demolished in 1946, the flagpole was placed beside a marker commemorating the CCC (see page 108) on the south side of a parking lot, which is now a part of the Christopher P. Dunne Memorial Visitor Center. (Courtesy of Malcolm Patterson Jr.)

Dressed in a sweater, peacoat, and woolen trousers, Malcolm Patterson poses at the top of a snowy hill called Wolf Rock in Breakheart. Even though this area is only 10 miles from Boston, standing on its rocky peaks gives visitors the feeling of being in a remote wilderness. (Courtesy of Malcolm Patterson Jr.)

Looking healthy and carefree, three CCC men, Malcolm Patterson, Pat Maderous, and Bill Travers, pose in front of camp trucks at Breakheart Hill Farm. The trucks were used to transport men to work and leisure activities in the surrounding area. Driving a truck was considered one of the better jobs in camp. (Courtesy of Malcolm Patterson Jr.)

Five CCC men, some with pitchforks, take a break from work. Malcolm Patterson is second from left. Nationwide, from 1933 to 1941, the CCC built over 125,000 miles of roads and 13,000 trails and strung 89,000 miles of telephone lines. They also completed erosion control projects for 40 million acres of farmland. (Courtesy of Malcolm Patterson Jr.)

The winters of the mid-1930s had plenty of snow to shovel, but, warm or cold weather, whatever activities they were engaged in, the men were always willing to stop for a picture. The unofficial motto of the CCC was "We can take it!" (Courtesy of Malcolm Patterson Jr.)

Dogs were popular pets in the CCC. Malcolm Patterson poses with CCC Company No. 1149's mascot, Rex, on the porch of the old 1890s Breakheart Hill Camp. During the late 1930s, the building was used for classrooms for CCC boys. (Courtesy of Malcolm Patterson Jr.)

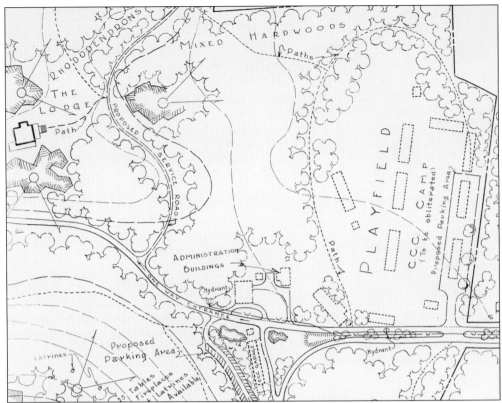

This is part of the 1939–1940 Breakheart Hill Layout Plan designed by Arthur Shurcliff for the MDC. It shows the CCC camp, garage, and administration buildings. All CCC buildings were targeted for demolition. However, the CCC camp was not razed until 1946, and Breakheart Hill Farm survived until 1973. The plan also shows the lodge (Breakheart Hill Camp) built by Benjamin Johnson and his partners in the 1890s as well as the water supply line into Breakheart. (Courtesy of DCR.)

The Recreation Hall was one of the most popular places in camp. Besides a large fieldstone fireplace, the building also housed a library, game room, and radio room. Outside, there was a baseball field and volleyball and tennis courts. Parcher baseball field still exists. (Courtesy of DCR.)

A rusty truck chassis still sits on the summit of Breakheart Hill. This was used to power a rope pull for the ski slope, developed by the CCC in 1936. The slope was improved by the MDC in the late 1950s, although never developed into a public ski area as proposed (see page 110). Two trails, the Breakheart Hill Trail and Fox Run Trail, now cross the former ski slope. At right is the ski slope looking west from Pinetops Road. (Authors' collection.)

Malcolm Patterson (left) and Wilbur King pose on Pinetops Road in 1936. In the late 1930s, motor vehicles were excluded from roads in Breakheart during blasting, construction, and grading activities. In 1961, when Breakheart Reservation was opened to the public, cars were permitted to drive on paved roads. However, the roads were again closed to motor vehicles in 1997 because of congestion and air pollution. (Courtesy of Malcolm Patterson Jr.)

Malcolm Patterson (left) and Pat Maderous strike a comical pose next to the barn at Breakheart Hill Farm. (Courtesy of Malcolm Patterson Jr.)

Wilbur King and Rex pose on the ice next to a rocky island in Upper Pond. The pond's dam, where water flows down a flume into Lower Pond, is visible in the distance. Many consider Upper Pond (called Silver Lake after 1960) to be one of the most beautiful ponds north of Boston. (Courtesy of Malcolm Patterson Jr.)

Wilbur King (left) and Bill Travers pose with two camp trucks in the snow. CCC records show that about 45,000 truck drivers were trained annually across the country. For many enrollees, operating a truck was their first driving experience. Once learned, they gained prestige. Training involved safety, maintenance, and mechanics, knowledge that served them well after their CCC years. (Courtesy of Malcolm Patterson Jr.)

Obviously good friends, four young men take a break from building trails to pose for a photograph. The CCC enrollees in each barracks were divided into work units called sections. Each section had 25 men, including a senior leader and assistant leader who were accountable for the men at work and in the barracks. (Courtesy of Forrest Howard.)

Members of CCC Company No. 1149 pose in front of their barracks in 1937. Most enrollees were between the ages 18 and 25 years and were unmarried. Their families were on local relief. After volunteering, they had to serve a minimum of six months, with the option of serving up to two years if they were unable to find outside employment. (Courtesy of DCR Archives.)

Every year, each CCC district published an annual report that contained photographs of the company and commanders and descriptions of work projects. A few men from each camp helped to write stories and choose images for these volumes, which were sold in CCC camp stores. This 1937 picture is part of a wide photograph, which was produced for one of the annuals, of the men of CCC Company No. 1149. (Photograph by T. Henry Merritt; courtesy of DCR Archives.)

This photograph of the CCC camp was taken looking south from Breakheart Hill Farm on Forest Street. Nationwide, the CCC was most active from April 1935 to March 1936 when enrollment peaked at 505,782 members in about 2,900 camps across the United States. By July 1936, membership had dropped to 350,000 enrollees in 2,019 camps. (Courtesy of DCR Archives.)

These photographs, taken in March 1936, show CCC men clearing snow and cutting trees along roads in Breakheart Reservation. Over several years, the men built more than six miles of roads. This entailed removing ledge using explosives, hauling away rock debris, grading road surfaces, and installing drainage culverts. (Both, courtesy of DCR Archives.)

01095

The above photograph shows a new road through Breakheart Reservation in the mid-1930s. CCC men constructed an elevated road surface beside a marsh and installed a culvert. By 1939, CCC men had paved 2.3 miles of park roads with tar and gravel, installed rustic guardrails, and built five parking areas for 271 cars. The photograph below shows the Forest Street entrance to Breakheart in June 1935. Three years later, this road was paved and widened to accommodate more traffic. (Both, courtesy of DCR Archives.)

This photograph shows a 12-man tree-spraying team on Forest Street in 1937. Beginning in 1935, nine tons of lead arsenate were sprayed along roads and trails in Breakheart to kill the eastern and forest tent caterpillars, canker worms, and gypsy moths. The cry of "Buggo!" could be heard through the woods in spring and summer when CCC crews began spraying. (Courtesy of DCR Archives.)

This Buggo Patrol is preparing to spray insecticides in the Breakheart woods. The gypsy moth, a species from Eurasia, was introduced in 1869 by Etienne Leopold Trouvelot of Medford, Massachusetts. He was experimenting with silk production when his caterpillars were accidentally released after a storm blew away their netting. (Courtesy of DCR Archives.)

Officials gather in front of the CCC infirmary during Parents' Day on June 17, 1936, to celebrate the first anniversary of the CCC camp. Officials include Frank Kane (far left); Clare Fechner, wife of Robert C. Fechner, national head of the CCC (fifth from left); Lauretta Bresnahan, state selecting agent for the CCC (patterned dress); Gov. James M. Curly (center); and General Rose (third from right). (Courtesy of Edward Patterson Jr.)

A wagon used to spray insecticides to control gypsy moths is parked in front of a large snow pile at Breakheart Hill Farm in 1937. Lead arsenate was first used in Massachusetts in 1892 for killing gypsy moths. A major problem with this insecticide was its tendency to adhere to apples. Lead arsenate was replaced by DDT in 1947. (Courtesy of Edward Patterson Jr.)

Harold Patterson of the CCC hoists a log while clearing trails in Breakheart Reservation in 1937. He was the uncle of Edward Patterson Jr., past president of the Saugus Historical Society, and ranger at Breakheart and Camp Nihan. (Courtesy of Edward Patterson Jr.)

This c. 1938 photograph shows a group of CCC men, including Forrest Howard (third from left), posing at a field kitchen on a hot, sunny day in Breakheart Reservation. (Courtesy of Forrest Howard Jr.)

Harold Patterson (right) and three fellow CCC enrollees stop work on Breakheart trails in 1938 to strike a playful pose for the camera. CCC men also planted many trees. Nationwide, from 1933 to 1942, they planted nearly three billion trees and are credited with restoring forests across the United States. (Courtesy of Forrest Howard Jr.)

On June 11, 1987, five decades after they had worked together to build trails and picnic areas and to fight gypsy moths and fires, members of CCC Company No. 1149 met for a reunion at Breakheart Reservation. Following their time in the CCC, most had served in World War II and returned home to work and raise families in Massachusetts. Forrest Howard is fourth from the right. (Courtesy of Forrest Howard Jr.)

This 1987 photograph shows former CCC member Ray Sargent standing next to the steps that had led to the CCC camp washroom at Breakheart Reservation. Sargent became an enrollee in 1933 and remained with the CCC until 1937. In an interview for the *Lynn Daily Item* on June 11, 1987, he said, "I learned how to control my own life. Every decision I made had to be my own." (Courtesy of Edward Patterson Jr.)

This stone marker was placed on the south side of the Christopher P. Dunne Memorial Visitor Center parking lot to commemorate the CCC and its role in developing Breakheart Reservation. Behind the marker is the flagpole that stood at the center of the CCC camp from 1935 to 1941. (Authors' collection.)

Six

MODERN AGE

The modern age for Breakheart began after World War II, when the federal government stopped using the reservation for military training. However, more than a decade passed before it was opened to the public.

In 1953, the MDC built a second entrance to Breakheart from the Wakefield side and, in 1959, proposed transforming the CCC ski slope on the eastern side of Breakheart Hill into a commercial operation. The plan was abandoned, but the old ski slope is still visible. In 1960, Lower Pond and Upper Pond were officially renamed Pearce and Silver Lakes. John Pearce had served as principal of Saugus High School, and Leo Silver had a dental office in Saugus for many years. That same year, the MDC hired noted Rockport artist Joseph Santoro to make sketches of the lakes and of designs for beach improvements and an ice-skating rink on the former site of the CCC camp.

In 1961, the MDC opened Breakheart to the public. It was summer, and families immediately flocked to the beach at Pearce Lake in their cars. The following year, the ice rink was built and dedicated to Saugus natives Walter and John Kasabuski. The brothers had died on the battlefield in Italy in 1945 within 12 days of one another.

Breakheart Hill Farm, which had stood for 200 years and was the scene of the heinous 1900 murder, fell into disrepair and was razed by the MDC in 1973. The hunting lodge belonging to Benjamin Johnson and his partners, which had been a bucolic retreat for so many prominent men of Lynn, was demolished by the MDC sometime between 1945 and 1950. Its foundation remains on the Lodge Trail.

In Breakheart's long and varied history, the CCC made the biggest mark on the modern reservation. Those young men, working for wages of $1 a day, preserved the forest and created the amenities people enjoy today, including its roads and hiking trails, dams and culverts, and pine groves and picnic areas.

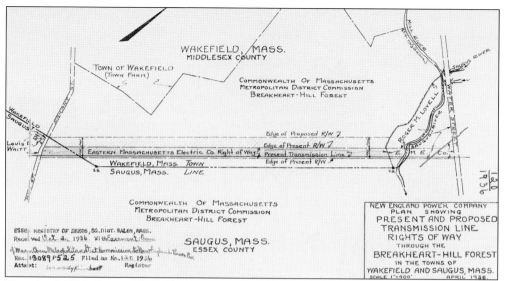

This April 1936 plan was drafted for the New England Power Company as part of a proposal to expand their right-of-way through Breakheart Hill Forest so that larger towers for high voltage lines could be built. This plan was approved by the state, and the new towers were built sometime after 1936. (Courtesy of South Essex Registry of Deeds.)

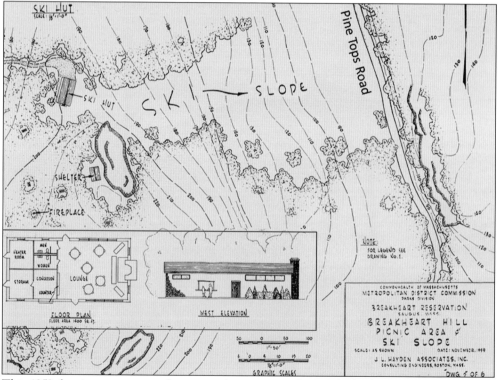

This 1959 drawing accompanied a proposal to improve the rough ski slope that the CCC had built on the eastern side of Breakheart Hill. Plans also included construction of a ski hut with a lounge, fireplace, and food concession. However, the MDC decided not to go forward with the plan. (Courtesy DCR Archives.)

This is a view of a gas pipeline looking north from the Saugus River Trail. In 1951, the Northeastern Gas Transmission Company laid out the 30-foot-wide pipeline right-of-way through the eastern half of Breakheart Reservation and the Cedar Glen Golf Club. (Authors' collection.)

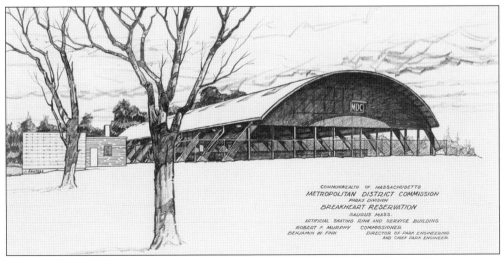

In 1960, noted Rockport artist Joseph L. C. Santoro (1908–1998) was commissioned by the MDC Parks Division to draw proposed improvements to Breakheart Reservation. This sketch shows a proposed covered ice rink on the site of the former CCC camp. In July 1961, the MDC initiated studies for a 185-by-85-foot rink that would cost $300,000. (Courtesy of DCR Archives.)

This Joseph Santoro drawing (above) shows an alternative design for an ice rink. This rendition includes both an indoor and outdoor rink. Below is the rink that was built in 1962 and named the Kasabuski Ice Arena in honor of Walter and John Kasabuski of Saugus. Both brothers died in action in Italy in 1945 while on patrol with the US Army 10th Mountain Division Company E. When John was shot on April 14, Walter rushed to his side but was unable to save him. Twelve days later, Walter was shot by a sniper and died instantly. In 1984, the arena underwent a $1-million renovation, including a new roof, locker rooms, and insulation, and reopened in January 1985. (Above, courtesy of DCR Archives; below, authors' collection.)

In 1960, Joseph Santoro sketched scenes of the Upper and Lower Ponds (renamed that year as Silver and Pearce Lakes) to entice more people to visit Breakheart Reservation. Below is Santoro's sketch of the proposed flume between the Upper and Lower Ponds. The earthen dam was first built in the 1890s. The flume was constructed by the CCC in 1937 and reconstructed after this sketch was made. (Both, courtesy of DCR Archives.)

Joseph Santoro drew this sketch of the proposed beach at Pearce Lake. After Breakheart Reservation opened to the public in 1961, thousands drove along Pine Tops Road to the beach, often resulting in traffic jams and air pollution. In the 1990s, the road was closed to motorized vehicles, and crowds now walk to the beach from both the Saugus and Wakefield entrances. The photograph below shows the beach as it looks today. (Above, courtesy of DCR Archives; below, authors' collection.)

Breakheart's Lower Pond was renamed Pearce Lake in 1960 after John Albert Weld Pearce (1893–1959), the son of a clergyman from Cornwall, England. Pearce graduated from Brown University in 1915 before teaching science and eventually serving as principal of Saugus High School for many years. In recognition of his service, Congressman Belden Bly Jr. of Saugus recommended that the Lower Pond be named after him. (Courtesy of Saugus Public Library.)

In this January 1965 photograph by Don Young, Boy Scouts from Wakefield Troop 701, from left to right, Tony deBeurs, Jack Schmidgall, Fred Allen and Bob Dawson, watch Robert Reen set up a nylon tent in Breakheart Reservation. Reen was a mountaineer and registered guide who often volunteered to instruct the troop about camping techniques under various weather conditions. (Courtesy of Don Young.)

Boy Scouts from Wakefield Troop 701 set up camp on a cold morning in December 1967. The Boy Scouts gathered branches from the forest to make tent supports. (Photograph by Don Young.)

Life Scout Fred Allen (left) of Wakefield Troop 701 shows his lantern to camping advisor Bob Reen after they hiked in Breakheart during one of three camping trips made in the winter 1965. (Photograph by Don Young.)

Dan Lynch and Tony deBeurs from Boy Scout Troop 701 warm themselves on a cold day in January 1965 while Scoutmaster Edward Schmidgall looks on. During this trip, the scouts used snowshoes to hike through the deep snow. (Photograph by Don Young.)

In this photograph by Don Young, Boy Scouts from Wakefield's Troop 701 discover that starting a fire without matches is a skill that takes practice. (Courtesy of Don Young.)

The North American beaver thrives in streams, ponds, and rivers. Before being hunted to near extinction for their fur, there were about 90 million beavers in the United States and Canada. They build lodges and dams, which can flood low areas, and they eat water lilies. Beavers also gnaw the bark of birch, poplar, and willow trees during the summer months. Beavers are becoming more common in Breakheart Reservation. The photograph above was taken beside the Saugus River near Camp Nihan, where many trees have been gnawed by beavers. The same beavers built a dam on the river that backed up water for about a mile. (Above, authors' collection; below, courtesy of DCR.)

The red fox originated in Eurasia and made its way to North America after the last glaciation. Red foxes feed mostly on small rodents. The DCR reported finding a den near Pine Tops Road containing remains of squirrel, duck, opossum, and muskrat. Outside breeding season, foxes live in vegetated areas and hunt mornings and evenings. When Breakheart was a private retreat, red fox would have been a popular animal to hunt, especially for its fur. The photograph below shows a fisher, an animal that has been trapped for its fur since the 18th century. Although it was thought to be gone from Breakheart, fisher tracks were found in snow west of Eagle Rock in 1992. Fishers feed on small animals, including porcupines, and fruits and mushrooms. In the 19th century, fishers nearly vanished from New England due to logging and fur trapping. (Both, courtesy of DCR.)

Boy Scouts of Troop 701 gain an appreciation for modern roads and snow-removal equipment as Marshall Winkler of Wakefield leads their horse and sled filled with camping equipment out of Breakheart Reservation during a blizzard in January 1965. (Photograph by Don Young.)

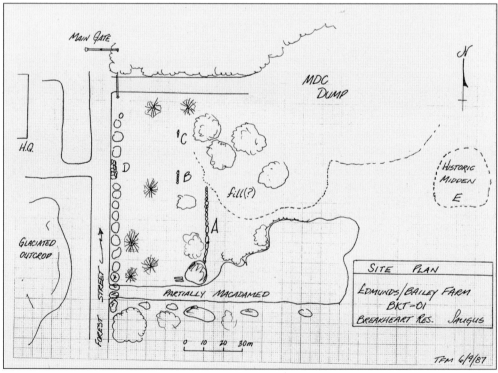

In June 1987, archaeologist Thomas F. Malstedt mapped the Breakheart Hill Farm site for the DCR. The barn, 1771 farmhouse, and utility buildings had been razed in 1973. Malstedt's map shows features that he observed, including stone walls, building foundations, and a historic midden, which contained 19th-century debris. (Courtesy of DCR Archives.)

120

The image above shows the first headquarters for Breakheart Reservation. Built in 1960, it was a simple, cinder-block structure containing offices, equipment storage areas, and a garage. After 40 years, it was covered by vines, which likely hastened deterioration of the mortar and contributed to ongoing problems with leaks. The photograph below shows the building being demolished in 2003. (Both, courtesy of DCR Archives.)

These 2003 photographs show the last stages of demolition of the first headquarters building. It was replaced by a parking lot for the Christopher P. Dunne Memorial Visitor Center. (Both, courtesy of DCR Archives.)

These 2004 photographs show the garage and visitor center under construction. The garage was constructed with twice as much storage space as the building it replaced and is used to store state vehicles. Students from the Northeast Vocational Technical School, which sits on former Breakheart Reservation property, helped with construction. (Both, courtesy of DCR Archives.)

Dozens came out on a chilly day in early 2004 to celebrate the ground-breaking of the Christopher P. Dunne Memorial Visitor Center. At the podium is Mark Falzone, state representative for Lynn, Lynnfield, Saugus, and Wakefield. Behind him are students from the Northeast Vocational Technical School, many of whom volunteered to help build the center. (Courtesy of DCR Archives.)

This photograph shows the Christopher P. Dunne Memorial Visitor Center under construction in May 2004. The main room of the visitor center has a large fieldstone fireplace and in winter attracts hikers and runners to stop by for a hot drink in front of a blazing fire. (Courtesy of DCR Archives.)

Christopher Dunne began working at Breakheart Reservation in high school and continued to work as a DCR employee after graduation. Outgoing and popular, Dunne greeted visitors to Breakheart until his sudden death in August 2003 at age 27. The photograph below shows Maria Caniglia, who assumed Dunne's position, in front of the Christopher P. Dunne Memorial Visitor Center in 2012. (Right, courtesy of DCR Archives; below, authors' collection.)

Breakheart Reservation sponsors many events each year. Two popular events are the New Year's Day Hike and the Tuff 10K trail race. DCR holds First Day hikes at many state parks to encourage year-round recreation. In the photograph above, Mike Nelson, supervisor of the DCR's North Region Park Rangers, leads a group along the Fox Run Trail on January 1, 2012. The 10K race is sponsored by the Saugus River Watershed Council and takes runners up and down Breakheart's highest peaks. At left is 2011 race winner, Matthew Carter of Saugus. Even with high heat and humidity, his winning time was 48 minutes 39 seconds, more than a minute faster than his 2010 finish. The 2011 race had 75 registered runners, 61 starters, and 60 finishers. (Above, authors's collection; left, photograph by Dan Burgess of the Saugus River Watershed Council.)

Standing on the summit of Castle Hill in Breakheart on July 20, 1963, Wakefield photographer Don Young captured this time-lapse image of a total eclipse of the sun. People throughout the northeastern United States and eastern Canada stopped their usual activities to witness this rare event, which had last occurred in 1959 and 1932. (Courtesy of Don Young.)

Foundations and steps of Breakheart Hill Camp and rhododendron garden still exist along the Lodge Trail, reminding us of the three businessmen from Lynn who decided to make their wilderness retreat here. It was this decision, made more than a century ago, which led to the preservation of Breakheart Reservation today. (Authors' collection.)

DISCOVER THOUSANDS OF LOCAL HISTORY BOOKS
FEATURING MILLIONS OF VINTAGE IMAGES

Arcadia Publishing, the leading local history publisher in the United States, is committed to making history accessible and meaningful through publishing books that celebrate and preserve the heritage of America's people and places.

Find more books like this at
www.arcadiapublishing.com

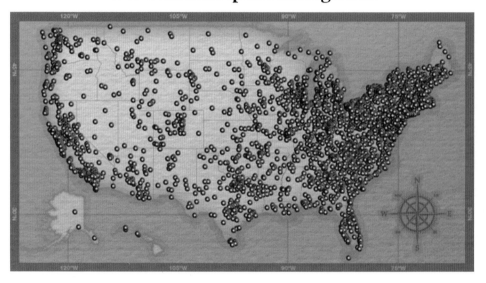

Search for your hometown history, your old stomping grounds, and even your favorite sports team.

Consistent with our mission to preserve history on a local level, this book was printed in South Carolina on American-made paper and manufactured entirely in the United States. Products carrying the accredited Forest Stewardship Council (FSC) label are printed on 100 percent FSC-certified paper.

MADE IN THE